Gilbert Phelps

STORY OF THE BRITISH MONARCHY

 Nile & Mackenzie Ltd — London

Frontispiece: The Imperial State Crown.

First published in Great Britain 1977 by
Nile & Mackenzie Limited
43 Dover Street
London WIX 3RE

© Nile & Mackenzie Limited 1977

ISBN 0 86031 020 5

The publishers would like to thank all those who have
helped in the production of this book. Acknowledgement
is also due to the British Information Services, British
Tourist Authority, and the National Portrait Gallery
for the supply of photographs used in the book.

Printed and bound in Singapore by FEP International Ltd.

STORY OF THE BRITISH MONARCHY

PREFACE

This short book, based on a series of scripts which I originally wrote for the BBC, does not of course pretend to be anything like a comprehensive history of the subject. At the same time it is hoped that it will provide, for general readers and students alike, a coherent and consecutive account of the origins and development of monarchical institutions in Britain, from the early days of tribal chieftains up to the modern concept of a constitutional monarchy operating within a democratic parliamentary state. In the process it is also hoped that the reader will, in so far as a limited angle of vision allows, obtain a bird's-eye view of most of the major events that have shaped the history of the British nation as a whole. After all, the story of the British monarchy is, inevitably, also the story of the British people.

Gilbert Phelps

CONTENTS

1	"God Save the Queen!"	1
2	The Royal Family	7
3	Legend and Fact	12
4	King Alfred and the Danes	22
5	Saxons, Danes — and Normans	28
6	The Norman Kings	40
7	The later Angevin Kings	47
8	Roses — Red, White and Tudor	56
9	Father and Daughter — the great Tudor Monarchy	63
10	The Stuarts — King versus Parliament	78
11	Towards a New Kind of Monarchy	87
12	The Hanoverians	96
13	Hanoverian to Windsor	109
14	The House of Windsor	129
	Epilogue	137
	Index	139

"God Save the Queen!" 1

N WESTMINSTER ABBEY on June 2nd, 1953, the most memorable moment of a memorable ceremony arrived, as the Archbishop of Canterbury (head of the established Church of England) took the Crown from its crimson cushion, held it aloft, and then placed it on the head of Queen Elizabeth II.

She had become the forty-second sovereign of England since the Norman Conquest of 1066, the sixth Sovereign Queen, and one of the seven remaining monarchs of Europe. Her subjects and citizens numbered five hundred and thirty-nine million. No monarch, moreover, had entered into the responsibilities of the office with a greater sense of dedication. One of the bishops attending the Coronation declared that one of the most moving experiences in his life had been the moment when, in accordance with one of the traditions of the ancient and symbolic coronation ritual, the young Queen had lifted the sword of state and laid it on the altar. He had felt that "she was putting her whole heart and soul to the service of her people".

There were foreign observers who found the situation puzzling. This was 1953. Since the war Britain had passed through a social revolution, much of it carried out by Labour governments. Inevitably the observers wondered whether this ancient ceremony could mean anything in the modern world. There could be no doubt, though, as to the enthusiasm of the crowds which thronged the Coronation route. No doubt, either, of the avid interest of those who stayed at home. The broadcasting of the coronation was a landmark in the history of the British Broadcasting Corporation. Its Listener Research Department reported that "to the on-the-spot viewers were added one half of the adult population who watched events on private or public television sets, and one third who listened on sound radio".

In other words, the vast majority of the population witnessed the coronation one way or another. And to these must be added the millions who followed the ceremony on radio or television in the countries of the British Commonwealth, and in many other parts of the world— including millions in the republic of the USA.

It was no mere flash in the pan, moreover. Eleven years later, support for the monarchy remained strong. A 1964 Mass Observation Survey, aimed at judging between republican and royalist feeling in Britain, revealed that outright critics of the monarchy amounted to no more than 13% of the total. The answers to specific questions were often fascinating, sometimes surprising, and always significant. In answer, for example, to the question which form of government was less likely to lead to extremes, 66% of those interviewed replied in favour of monarchy. Even the question "Which is more likely to be democratic?" received a 50% 'vote' for the monarchy, with 35% for a republic.

When it came to deciding which form of government was better from the point of view of political relations with other countries, 64% declared for the monarchy, as opposed to only 23% for a republic. And in dealing with questions of a more intangible (though equally important) nature, support for the monarchy became overwhelming. Thus 77% believed that the monarchy was more likely to further the religious life of the nation—and a massive 84% that a monarchy would have a better effect on the country's moral and family life.

It seems evident, then, that the monarchy in Britain, whether it is a Labour or a Conservative government in power, is popular with the vast majority of the people. What is more surprising, perhaps, is that it is almost certainly more popular today, in the era of the welfare state, when many of the old class divisions and privileges have withered away, than at any time during the past two hundred years. In part this is due to the character and personality of the Queen herself, and to the closeness of her contacts with her people in many spheres and walks of life. It is, after all, the small human actions that count with ordinary people rather than the grand political and constitutional issues, and Dorothy Laird, one of the Queen's biographers, has reported a little incident which excellently illustrates the simple personal kindliness which the Queen so often displays:

On one occasion, when a newspaper reporter whom she had formerly trusted had published a malicious and inaccurate article about her, one of her ladies-in-waiting said with emphasis that she intended to 'cut' that reporter at the next available opportunity. 'Oh, don't do that,' exclaimed the Queen spontaneously. 'He is a nice man!'

What, though, is the position of the monarchy within the British constitution? As it *is* a constitutional monarchy, the sovereign exercises no direct power. Political power resides entirely with the government of the day, and the government of the day is the ministry which commands a majority in the House of Commons. The Queen has no real say in its composition. When it comes to the appointment or dismissal of ministers, the Prime Minister 'advises' the Queen, but in effect it is he who carries them out. It is on his 'advice', too, that Parliament is dissolved, so that a general election can take place. When the Prime Minister himself resigns, the Queen must send for the Leader of the Opposition, or whatever statesman is likely to be able to form a new government which will enjoy the confidence of the House of Commons; though in this case, too, she would usually consult the outgoing Prime Minister as to the choice of his successor.

Fundamental to the whole concept of British constitutional monarchy is the absolute political neutrality of the sovereign. The Queen, of course, has her own private opinions like anyone else, but publicly she has no political views in the party sense of the term. Her politics, officially speaking, are those laid down by the government of the day. This principle has gradually embedded itself into our system ever since the British monarchy began to evolve into a constitutional one. More than three hundred years ago, for example, King Charles II said, "My words are my own, but my actions are my Ministers'."

The Queen's public actions, therefore, are in no way determined by her personal wishes. On the face of it this may seem an impossibly frustrating situation for her — but it does at least mean that she cannot be involved in any controversy that may arise out of those actions. She is truly outside and above the political arena. The indirect powers of the sovereign, however — though perhaps the word 'influence' would be more appropriate — are very considerable. It must be remembered that the British constitution, unlike so many others, is not a written one. It is, in consequence, both complex and unique. To quote Professor William Robson: "many relics of past ages survive . . . long after they have lost original significance and been overlaid by modern arrangements . . . the system of government contains many inconsistencies and anomalies arising from changes in tradition and emphasis which are tolerated only because the opportunities they offer formally are not pressed to their logical conclusion. The constitution depends for its successful working on numerous understandings and adjustments of an informal character."

3

Now it happens quite often that the only person in a position to exercise such understandings and adjustments is the sovereign. An outstanding instance took place in 1923 when King George V — the present Queen's grandfather — came to the conclusion (advised by his ministers) that henceforth the Prime Minister must be a member of the House of Commons (the lower house of Parliament). There is no law that says this must be the case, but the King having once agreed to the principle, it has become accepted, and no politician would dream of reversing it. There have been instances of a similar nature, and it could be argued very forcibly that a system that depends so much on unwritten agreements can best be preserved by an hereditary monarchy, because it alone, being outside the political rat race, has no axe to grind.

The vital part played by the sovereign in the working of a system which seems sprawling and amorphous, but which history has shown to possess an organic unity and vitality of its own, has been commented on by Sir Charles Petrie, historian of the British monarchy:

> The man-in-the-street is inclined to take for granted the smooth running of the constitution ... but this is only achieved by eternal vigilance, not least on the part of the Crown, which often has to moderate the bitterness of party strife to achieve this result.

The monarchy, in fact, may be seen as a tree whose roots spread in all directions, holding the soil together. How inextricably the position of the sovereign is involved in the whole texture of the nation's life can be seen in a few random but salient facts. It is the Crown, for example, which appoints, on ministerial advice, most of the highest administrative and judicial officers; the Royal Prerogative confers upon the Queen the exclusive right to conduct international affairs with foreign countries, to make peace and war, to appoint and receive ambassadors and other diplomatic representatives and to make treaties; the Queen is commander-in-chief of the Navy, the Army, and the Air Force; she is the Governor of the Established Church; she is "the fountain of honour", and it is she, therefore, who confers all titles; she can, in consultation with her ministers, exercise the "prerogative of mercy" in pardoning prisoners; and it is she who is charged in law with the guardianship of infants and lunatics. All these matters and many others are conducted in her name by her ministers and their officials. In addition, all Acts of Parliament require her consent, and until this is given they cannot become law. It is true that in all these functions the Queen must be guided by the government of the day, but she is the undoubted linchpin without which the whole system would fall apart.

There are four advantages that stand out above all others in this system. The first is that the position of the Queen goes a long way to

4

eliminating those transfer of power crises that have been common in many other parts of the world. In the second place, the fact that all judges are appointed by the Crown makes it almost impossible for the British judicial system to become the pawn of party political differences. Thirdly, the fact that the Queen is the commander-in-chief of the armed forces makes it virtually impossible for any politician to gain control of them, or for any commander to seize power. And, perhaps most important of all, sudden coups or attempts of would-be dictators to seize power would in all likelihood be aborted by the sheer complexity of the constitutional position and the place of the sovereign at its centre. The Queen may not have power in the crude sense — but she makes it well nigh impossible for anyone else to usurp it.

The Queen also possesses three rights — they are so called in order to avoid the use of the word 'powers' — which are of incalculable importance. Walter Bagehot, a great nineteenth-century constitutional historian, defined them as follows: "The right to be consulted, the right to encourage, the right to warn."

Every affair of state, no matter how small, must be reported to the Queen and no provision can become law without her signature. Often, too, it may well turn out that the Queen's experience and memory of affairs are more complete than those of her ministers because while they come and go according to the political pendulum, she is the fixed point that is always there. As the recipient, by right, of all state papers and as the hostess of visiting statesmen, she may be in a position to have a fuller picture, a wider overall perspective. In consequence she is often able to draw her ministers' attention to circumstances that have been overlooked or forgotten — and thus either to encourage them to go forward or to warn them to draw back.

But if the Queen is a link between succeeding ministers of different parties, even more so is she *the* link with the British past. An unwritten constitution like that of Great Britain, depends for its successful operation on a central repository of its traditions — and to a large extent that repository is the monarchy. As Clement (later Lord) Attlee, Prime Minister of the first Labour governments after the war, said: "A conscientious constitutional monarch is a strong element of stability and continuity in our Constitution." And certainly Queen Elizabeth II has proved herself to be nothing if not conscientious.

One of the main difficulties in explaining how the British constitution works lies in the fact that it depends to such a large extent on intangible relationships which are perhaps more easily *felt* than analysed. But these emotional factors are probably as important as the purely constitutional ones for the mass of the British people. What struck many observers at the present Queen's coronation was the way in which 5 the British public seemed to identify itself with the occasion, so that it took on all the deeper vibrations of a truly national — almost, one might say, a tribal — gathering. And the then Prime Minister, Sir Winston Churchill, speaking at the Coronation luncheon in Westminster, on May 27th, 1953, summed up the difference between the two time-scales — the fluctuating and temporal one of party politics, and the timeless one represented by the monarch — in two sentences: "A great battle is lost: Parliament turns out the Government. A great battle is won — crowds cheer the Queen."

The Royal Family 2

 HE HEAD of any family can be helped or hindered by its other members. The outstanding feature of the present British royal family has, by and large, been its impressive unity. As Sir Charles Petrie has humorously put it, the Queen's family

> is now a definite asset rather than the liability its members used to be in the days when a wise monarch kept them under close observation, if not actually in the Tower itself.

The consequence is that each of them plays a part in bringing the monarchy to the notice of the people when the Sovereign cannot herself be present in person, and so helps to make the Crown a reality to millions.

The Queen herself is inevitably in a special position. It is one of awe-inspiring responsibility. It is also one of frequent loneliness, for the attitude of the public is often ambivalent. On the one hand it expects royal personages in the modern world to be democratic and human. But on the other hand, with one part of its mind it also clings to the traditional picture of the monarch as someone almost inhumanly dedicated and aloof.

It was an intimidating task, in fact, that the young Queen was called upon to face when she ascended the throne. It was the more difficult because it was a time of uncertainty. For one thing, the old Empire was rapidly breaking up. This had indeed been signalized by an innovation in the proclamation of the Queen's accession in 1952. For she was proclaimed, in each of the self-governing countries of what 7 used to be called the British Empire, as Queen of that particular country, and the abandonment of the old principle of the indivisibility of the Crown was confirmed by statute in 1953 (in time for the Coronation) when a new description "Head of the Commonwealth", was inserted among the royal titles to allow for the inclusion of republics like India and Pakistan.

It was not long before Queen Elizabeth II revealed that she had inherited all her father's passionate devotion to duty. She is conscientious, at times over-conscientious; she plans her work with painstaking care, and carries it out with unflinching application. At a time of crisis an eminent Church leader declared:

> I was just amazed at her — the strength and ability of her mind, her sure grasp of affairs, her sense of real concern and compassion for her people . . .

The manner in which the Queen tackles the vast amount of paper work with which she is confronted almost daily has been particularly commented on. It is well known that she reads and digests it all with great thoroughness and patience, spending many hours on it; and a member of her household reports that she has "an amazing way of sucking facts out of the dullest document".

Of course, she also has a vast number of official and semi-official engagements, from the State Opening of Parliament to attending an international Rugby football match at Twickenham. In addition, she is probably the most widely travelled monarch in British history. Some of her tours have been staggering in their scope. The six-month Commonwealth Tour of 1953, for example, involved the Queen and her husband in 30,890 kilometres of travel by sea, 27,630 by air, 5,760 by car, and 2,400 by train.

Like her father King George VI, the Queen is a very shy person, who is not immediately or exuberantly outgoing; but as someone close to the royal household has observed:

> The Queen creates an atmosphere of trust and sincerity around her . . . She has outstanding qualities of steadfastness. She never takes up a . . . person on impulse, to drop them again just as lightly. She is a serene person in a firmly-rooted setting.

And one of the artists who have painted her portrait was struck by the inner tranquillity which enabled her to maintain her pose before the canvas without either affectation or fidgeting.

None of this implies, however, that the Queen is in any way forbidding. One of the officials at the Palace has remarked that "a lot of laughing goes on in this house". In fact, the Queen has a strong sense of humour. She enjoys the company, for instance, of her favourite comedians, Spike Milligan and Peter Sellers, two of the moving spirits in a famous radio comedy series known as 'The Goons'—and in April 1965, the *Daily Mirror* reported:

> Milligan and Sellers had supper with the Queen. It was the zaniest Royal Birthday party ever—the night the Queen celebrated her birthday with a couple of Goons.

The Queen also takes great pleasure in the theatre, the ballet, music (especially singing) and in the collection of pictures in her various residences. But it is in country pursuits that she finds the greatest relaxation. Everybody knows of her love for her Corgi dogs and her passion for horses and racing (though she has not the least interest in gambling). But what is not so commonly known is that she is something of an expert in the breeding of horses, their training and care.

In all spheres of life she finds constant support from her husband, the Duke of Edinburgh. This was the title conferred on Philip by King George VI before he married the Princess Elizabeth (as she then was) on November 20th, 1947. In 1957, however, Philip was also granted the titular dignity of Prince of the United Kingdom, and so is now more generally known as Prince Philip. He is himself of royal birth—the only son of Princess Alice (a great-granddaughter of Queen Victoria), and of Prince Andrew of Greece. While the Greek royal family were in exile in England from 1923 to 1935, Prince Philip was educated at Cheam Preparatory School, near London, at Gordonstoun (in Scotland), and at the Royal Naval College, Dartmouth, serving in the Royal Navy during the war. He became a British citizen in 1947, renouncing all his Greek titles, and adopting his mother's family name of Mountbatten.

Comparisons have often been made between Prince Philip and Prince Albert (the Prince Consort to Queen Victoria) though not as far as popularity is concerned—for Prince Albert, in marked contrast to Prince Philip, often incurred the disfavour and even hostility of the general public. It is in his very real interest and knowledge of science, industry and technology that Prince Philip most resembles the Prince Consort. He has impressed specialists in these fields, and has addressed the Royal Society. He has made it his special concern to promote technological research and the modernization of British industry. In this respect he has often been a speaker of home-truths, as when he told a gathering of manufacturers: "It is no good shutting your eyes, saying 'Britain is best' three times a day and expecting it to be so." It is no secret in fact that Prince Philip enjoys making speeches, and he has also made a number of extremely adept appearances on BBC Television.

One of his other great interests is the Outward Bound Movement. The idea that adventure and outdoor activity, in the service of others, should figure prominently in education originated with Dr Kurt Hahn, the distinguished educationist and refugee from Nazi Germany who founded Gordonstoun. In 1946 the Outward Bound Trust was launched, with Prince Philip as its patron and moving spirit. There are now six centres which give residential courses in sea and mountain rescue work to young people of both sexes and every social class — and the Duke of Edinburgh Awards for outstanding feats of endurance and self-reliance are much coveted honours. Prince Philip was also one of the pioneers in the cause of conservation of wild species in danger of extinction. He is a keen yachtsman and an almost fanatical polo player.

He owes much of his popularity to the fact that, through sheer force of personality, he has steadily eroded some of the more irksome barriers between the monarchy and the public. It is largely due to him that much of the red tape and protocol surrounding the court has been relaxed. His easy and self-confident manner has gone down well in an increasingly democratic age, and the fact that it is attended by a certain impatience with official humbug and sometimes laced with a pungent and forth-right turn of phrase, has enhanced rather than detracted from its effectiveness. There is little doubt that the performance of the Queen's public duties has benefited from the relaxed bearing of her husband. Nevertheless, hers is the more difficult task, and her greatest triumph perhaps is in maintaining the balance between human and personal qualities, and the dignity and necessary distance demanded by her office. And in her relations with the public her husband has generally proved the perfect foil and complement.

This more free-and-easy attitude towards the monarchy has, more-over, been transferred to the royal children. The Queen and Prince Philip were determined that all of them, Charles the heir-apparent included, should live as normal a life as possible, and not be thrust into public duties before they were ready for them. Thus Prince Charles went to the same schools as his father, and then, like him, entered the Royal Navy. When he served on HMS *Norfolk* he lived the normal life of a junior officer, insisting on being called Charles by his fellow-officers, performing his naval duties with enthusiasm, and taking an accomplished part in ward-room theatricals and entertainments.

Like his mother, Prince Charles is fond of the Goons, and has held his own in bouts of zany comedy repartee with Spike Milligan. Besides his naval commission, Prince Charles also has his pilot's wing, and he enjoys both flying and driving. He is keenly interested in archaeology, which he studied for a year at Cambridge University, and has taken part in several 'digs'. He is also an enthusiastic performer on the cello. Like his father, he shows great ease and unaffected charm at the microphone and before the television cameras. What has most struck observers, perhaps, is that he has inherited both his father's charm and frankness, and his mother's combination of gentleness and steadiness of purpose. By now, of course, he has had more than a taste of what lies before him. His first really major introduction to public life took place in 1969, when at the age of twenty-one, he was invested as Prince of Wales, and presented to the Welsh people by his mother, at a ceremony held at Caernarvon Castle. He is the twenty-first holder of the title. He has admitted that the realization that he was heir to the throne was "something which dawns on you with the most ghastly inexorable sense". Nevertheless he will benefit from the relaxation of the more rigid aspects of monarchy that have taken place in his lifetime.

One of the symptoms of this relaxation has been the increasing number of marriages between members of the royal family and commoners. The marriage of the Queen's sister, Princess Margaret, to Anthony Armstrong-Jones (who was created Lord Snowdon) in May 1960 attracted particular interest. The public remembered with sympathy her earlier romance with the Battle of Britain pilot Group Captain Peter Townsend, whom she renounced, in large part because of the continuing objections of the Church of England to marriage between a royal person with special constitutional and public duties to perform, and a partner whose previous marriage had ended in divorce. Other marriages between members of the royal family and commoners have been that of the Duke of Kent to Katherine Worsley, daughter of a Yorkshire baronet, in 1961 and that of Princess Alexandra to the Hon. Angus Ogilvie, the son of the Earl of Airlie, in 1963. Earlier the Earl of Harewood (son of King George VI's sister Mary, the Princess Royal) was married to Marion Stein, a concert pianist. Then in November 1973, Princess Anne married the Olympic Gold Medallist Captain Mark Phillips (a country squire, and a descendant of the Duke of Marlborough).

What is of outstanding importance about these marriages is the way in which they have further extended the range of classes, regions, talents, and professions encompassed by the royal family. Lord Snowdon, for instance, is a distinguished photographer and designer and both he and Princess Margaret have had close contacts with artistic and theatrical circles. Even before his first marriage, Lord Harewood was one of the country's leading musicologists, a specialist in opera, and author of books on music. The Duke of Kent's wife belongs to the county squire-archy. There are critics, of course, who wish that the monarchy played a more active part in the artistic and cultural life of the nation, but it is no exaggeration to say that from the throne at the centre, ripples spread out far and wide into the modern world.

3 Legend and Fact

HE DIFFERENT PEOPLES who, in past times, lived in or colonized the island of Britain — Ancient Britons, Picts, Scots, Anglo-Saxons and Normans — have all survived and mingled, to form the British people of today. Historians of the British monarchy sometimes maintain that the blood royal of each of these peoples, even the most ancient, also survives in the British royal family today.

Some of the evidence for such an assertion — as with most claims made for ancient dynasties — must, of course, lie in the realm of legend and tradition, rather than in that of proven historical fact. There is little doubt, though, that Queen Elizabeth II can trace her royal ancestry for well over a thousand years, while some of the traditions relating to still earlier times cannot be dismissed out of hand.

It used to be assumed that the Celts — or Ancient Britons, as the pre-Roman inhabitants are usually known — were savage barbarians. The work of archaeologists in recent years, however, has shown that in many

---

Page 13: A special Jubilee portrait of the Queen, taken in 1976, after the official State Opening of Parliament.

Pages 14–15: The Queen at the Trooping of the Colour ceremony, a spectacular military pageant held annually on her official birthday.

Page 16: The Queen at the State Opening of Parliament, during which she addresses both Houses of Parliament from the Throne.

cases they had reached a high level of civilization. One hundred and fifty years before the birth of Christ, for instance, the south British tribes had a gold coinage of their own, imitated from the gold *stater* of the kings of Macedon, and beautiful specimens of the art and craftsmanship of the Ancient Britons can be seen in the British Museum. This civilization was centred upon the royal houses.

It was because the Ancient British tribes of southern England sent help to the closely related Gauls of northern France that the great Roman general Julius Caesar, who was at war with the Gauls, invaded Britain in 55 BC. He took a small force and moved barely sixteen kilometres inland from the neighbourhood of Dover. The following year he returned with a larger force—and it is now that the first of the patriot kings enters the British tradition. He was no legend, however, because it is known from the Roman historians that his name was Cassivelaunus, king of a powerful tribe named the Catuvellauni. The Ancient Britons put up a stout resistance. To quote the famous historian Sir George Trevelyan:

> ... the yellow haired, athletic aristocracy of the Celts in their scythed chariots clattered down the war-ways of the battle like heroes of Homer, in a manner disconcerting even to the veterans of the Roman Tenth Legion.

Nevertheless, Roman discipline and organization prevailed; but after a while the Romans again withdrew, and it was nearly a hundred years before they returned. In the meantime another king of the Catuvellauni entered British royal history and legend. His name was Cunobelin, or Cymbeline, and he reigned from AD 5 to 40. He increased the hegemony of the Catuvellauni over the rival tribes to such an extent that he styled himself on his gold coinage *Rex Brittonum* (King of Britain). The use of Latin is symptomatic of the good relations which Cymbeline cultivated with the Roman Emperors Augustus and Tiberius and of his encouragement of Roman traders, craftsmen, and of Roman civilization generally. His capital (and royal mint) was first of all near the present city of St Albans, and then at the site of modern Colchester—but it is almost certain that he also founded the city of London.

London at any rate was in existence, though still in vestigial form, when in AD 43, under the Emperor Claudius, the Romans set about the conquest of the island in earnest. Before long they had conquered nearly the whole of what is now England and had advanced into Wales. But in AD 61, while the Roman legions were still busy fighting in Wales, a serious rebellion broke out among the tribes of the south-east, led by the Iceni and their queen Boadicea. The inhabitants of the Roman settlements at Colchester, London and Verulanium (near the present-day St Albans) were put to the sword. The Roman legions hurried back from Wales and suppressed the revolt, but the golden-haired Queen Boadicea, charging into battle on a chariot with scythes on its axles, has remained one of our great national heroines, whose name is known to every English school-child. The fact that she took poison rather than submit to the Romans added to her glory and perhaps helped in the creation of a mystique of monarchy.

The Romans occupied England and most of Wales (apart from some of the mountainous regions which were never subdued) for nearly three hundred years. They established Roman civilization and, in the reign of the Emperor Constantine, introduced Christianity. But the fierce warriors from the Baltic and North Sea coast of Germany, who began to raid England as the Roman Empire fell into decay, were pagans. After the last Roman legions were withdrawn in AD 407, to help defend Rome itself against other barbarian hordes, these raids turned into systematic waves of invasion. The main bodies of invaders were the Jutes, who colonized Kent; the Angles, who settled in East Anglia and along the north-east coast — and from whom the name England is derived; and the Saxons, whose name lives on in Essex, Sussex and Wessex — the lands, that is, of the East Saxons, South Saxons and West Saxons.

During the period of the invasions there was a temporary revival of the Ancient Britons, or Celts. They appear to have for the most part absorbed the surviving Romano-Britons, or to have joined in alliance with them, and to have organized large areas of the country under the leadership of various head-kings. Little is known of this period historically, but it is rich in legend and tradition. Nearly all British children still learn the old nursery rhyme:

> Old King Cole was a merry old soul,
> A merry old soul was he.
> He called for his pipe, he called for his bowl,
> And he called for his fiddlers three.

King Cole, or Coel, was a semi-legendary Celtic king who, about the year 400, ruled over a large part of Britain. Gradually, though, the Celts were pressed back by the Anglo-Saxon invaders. Many of them retreated into Wales, taking the Christian faith with them, and King Cole is supposed to have been the ancestor of the Welsh kings, who adopted a red dragon as their badge. Among them was King Cadwaladr the Blessed. From him the Tudor line is supposed traditionally to have descended — and the present Queen, of course, has Tudor blood in her veins. The traditional emblematic leek of King Cadwaladr is in fact still worn by her Majesty's Welsh Guards, while from her ancestral dragon badge,

the Queen still names one of her pursuivants (hereditary Officers of the

College of Arms) *Rouge Dragon*. Other Celts retreated far west to Cornwall, which still has a special identity, recognized in one of Prince Charles's titles — Duke of Cornwall.

The Picts, who lived in the northern part of England and the southern regions of Scotland, were never conquered, either by the Romans or by the Saxons. On the contrary, they continually invaded England themselves, and the Roman Emperor Hadrian, who visited Britain in AD 121, ordered the building of a wall, backed up by a system of fortifications, right across the northern neck of England to try and keep them out. Much of this wall still remains, together with remains of the fortifications. The Scots, living farther north, were a Celtic race different from the Picts, but in time their royal lines merged. One of their princesses married the hereditary Great Steward of Scotland — and her descendants were known as the Stewarts, later spelt 'Stuarts'. As the result of a dynastic marriage a Stuart king eventually became King of England as well as of Scotland, and Queen Elizabeth II is his direct descendant. The ancient Scottish kings also inherited the isles of Bute and Arran, off the west coast of Scotland, which originally had kings of their own. Today Prince Charles still has among his titles those of Great Steward of Scotland and Lord of the Isles.

The greatest and most persistent body of legends about the period after the withdrawal of the Romans from Britain centres on King Arthur. He is represented in these legends as a great Christian hero, who led the British (or Celtic) chieftains against the pagan invaders, and defeated them in twelve great battles, the last of them about the year 500. But no one knows for certain whether or not he really existed or who exactly he was, though Professor R.G. Collingwood, a famous historian of early Britain, is of the opinion that he was possibly: "the last of the Romans; the last to understand Roman ideas and use them for the British people."

Among these ideas was probably that of organizing cavalry after the Roman pattern. In most of the legends Arthur is attended by knights — known as Knights of the Round Table, because Arthur insisted on sitting with them at a round table so that no one would be at the head, and all would appear equal. Eventually Arthur was apparently defeated and killed, in a treacherous revolt among his own people. But many believed that he was taken to a kind of magical paradise from which he would one day return to help the British people in a time of great need. The site of an ancient castle, in the west country, which tradition claims to be that of Arthur's palace, is now being excavated by archaeologists.

The Arthurian legends exercised a powerful influence on the mystique of British royalty for many years. When, for example, an Italian historian in the reign of Henry VIII dismissed the whole Arthurian story as nonsense, considerable national resentment was aroused. The odds, in 19 fact, are that Arthur himself did exist, but the important point about the Arthurian legends is that they embody the ideal — heroic, chivalric, and Christian — which traditionally lies behind the British monarchy.

To turn from the mists of legend surrounding the early invasions of the Anglo-Saxons to historical fact, although the western half of England still remained in Celtic hands, in the course of the sixth century invaders had settled down to establish a chain of separate but contiguous kingdoms. And it is with these Anglo-Saxon kingdoms that the continuous historical record of England begins — and with it the history of our monarchy.

The word 'king' itself, indeed, is derived from the Anglo-Saxon *cyning*. This word is itself probably related to 'kin', and indicates that the ruler concerned stood at the head of his kindred or tribe. In other words, kings were in origin merely tribal chieftains. For a long time, in fact, there were a large number of them. But gradually seven — the kings of Wessex, Sussex, Kent, Essex, East Anglia, Mercia, and Northumbria — emerged as the most powerful. In the course of time three of these — Wessex, Mercia and Northumbria — began to vie for domination over their smaller neighbours, with first one kingdom, then another, holding sway over the rest. It was the first step towards the eventual unification of the country under a single royal house.

The process was given further impetus by the reintroduction of Christianity by missionaries from Europe, and from Celtic Wales, Cornwall and Ireland. Christianity provided (apart from the more important spiritual issues) a cohesive and civilizing force which most of the Saxon kings eventually came to recognize, although there were a number of relapses to paganism calling for fresh efforts from the missionaries. In some cases it was the queens who were largely instrumental in bringing about the conversion to Christianity. When, for example, Augustine, despatched from Rome by Pope Gregory the Great, arrived in Kent in 597, he found a staunch ally in Bertha, the wife of King Ethelbert of Kent, who was herself a Frankish Christian. It was St Augustine (or Austin) who founded the see of Canterbury in Kent (at this time London was still resolutely pagan) and became its first Archbishop.

Similarly, Ethelburga, a convert of Augustine's, on her betrothal to Edwin, the pagan King of Northumbria, in 625, helped to bring about his conversion, and Augustine's Roman associate Paulinus, who had accompanied Ethelburga northwards, became the first Archbishop of York.

The kingdom of Northumbria stretched from the river Humber to the Firth of Forth, thus taking in the south-eastern part of the lowlands of Scotland which later came to be known as Lothian — and it was King Edwin who built, on the now famous rock, the fortification which formed the northernmost stronghold of Saxondom in Britain, and called it

"Edwin's Burg", which later became Edinburgh, the capital of Scotland.

Northumbria's power, however, was broken by the pagan King Penda of Mercia, in alliance with the Christian Welsh under their king Cadwallon, and he extended his own territory to the lands beyond the river Severn. Northumbria was now no longer a contender for supremacy, although it retained its independence and remained a great centre of art, literature, and religion throughout the period of the great scholar and monk known as the Venerable Bede and of St Cuthbert, prior of the famous island monastery of Lindisfarne.

The struggle now lay between Mercia and Wessex, and the next crucial step on the long road towards the unification of England under a single monarchy came when Edgar, King of Wessex, defeated the Mercians (now also converted to Christianity) at the battle of Ellandune in 825 and decisively established the supremacy of his own kingdom. Edgar has been called "the first king of all England". That is an exaggeration, inasmuch as Edgar's sovereignty was loose, undefined and incomplete. On the other hand, it was sufficiently firmly based to give rise to something approaching genuine institutions of central and local government, which made the English monarchy amongst the most mature in Europe of its time. Even at this early stage, indeed, many of the features of the modern British monarchy were already present in embryo. It should also be noted that in the Saxon Witan, or assembly of wise men, which had the power of making laws and even on occasion of deposing kings and electing new ones, some historians have seen the seeds of future Parliamentary institutions. In addition, it is from Edgar that the genealogists trace Queen Elizabeth II's royal descent.

4 King Alfred and the Danes

UST AS WESSEX was emerging as the most powerful of the Anglo-Saxon kingdoms of England, new waves of invaders began to arrive. They were Scandinavians, who came from what are now Denmark and Norway, though they are usually referred to as the Danes or Vikings. They began by attacking the other English kingdoms — and this had important consequences for the future of English unity and of the English monarchy. For as the dynasties of Northumbria, Mercia and East Anglia, and with them their cultural and religious triumphs, were in turn destroyed by the invaders, Wessex was left to shoulder the burden alone — and so her kings became in many important respects the genuine leaders of the whole nation.

The distinctive Viking warships, with their long curved prows, were already thrusting in strength into the creeks and harbours of England during the reign of King Egbert of Wessex, who died in 839. His son, King Aethelwulf, was called upon to sustain the full fury of the invaders, illustrated in this laconic extract from the *Anglo-Saxon Chronicle* (compiled by monks attached to the court of Wessex) recalling the year 843:

> King Aethelwulf fought at Carlhampton against thirty-five ships' companies, and the Danes had possession of the place of slaughter.

But in the hour of England's need there came to the throne of Wessex, in the year 871, Aethelwulf's son King Alfred, one of the greatest of all English monarchs.

From the beginning and while still a youth, Alfred was forced to be

The Anglo-Saxon Kings of England (802–1066)

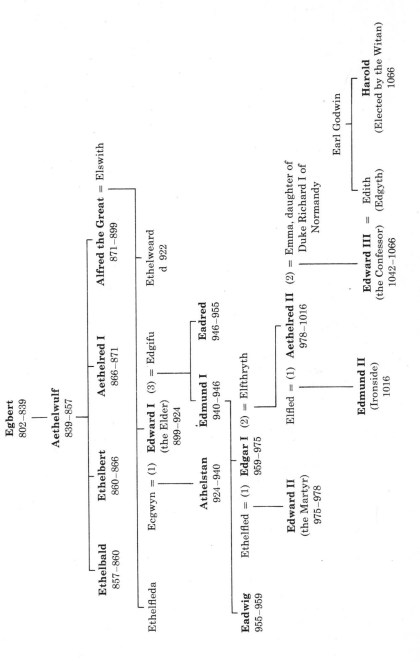

a warrior king in spite of the fact that he was delicate in health and a scholar by temperament — though his grim experiences of battle never soured his gentle qualities.

By this time the Danes had already settled in eastern England (where their presence is still marked in numerous placenames and even in the physical appearance of many of the inhabitants), had conquered much of the rest of England, and were driving southwards into Wessex. In the year of his accession Alfred checked them in nine battles south of the river Thames. He had saved his kingdom, but the danger was by no means over, and the great crisis of Alfred's life came in the year 878. At the time there was an uneasy peace, and Alfred was not expecting disaster. And then, his biographer and contemporary, the Welshman Bishop Asser, relates:

> ... the Danish host went secretly in midwinter when Alfred and his followers felt secure from attack ... to Chippenham, and rode over Wessex and occupied it, and drove a great part of the inhabitants oversea, and reduced the greater part of the rest, except Alfred the king; and he with a small company moved under difficulties through woods and into inaccessible places in marshes.

The most inaccessible of these places was the lake-isle of Athelney in Somerset (one of the counties in the west of England). Many stories of this period survive into history and legend. The most famous of them describes how King Alfred, his clothing torn and stained by battle, sheltered in a cowherd's cottage on Athelney. The cowherd's wife had some cakes baking before the fire, and when she went out for a while she told her mysterious visitor to keep an eye on them, but he fell deep in thought about his plans for turning the tables on the Danes, and forgot all about the cakes. When she came back the cowherd's wife found them burned to a cinder — and boxed the King's ears in her exasperation. Another tradition relates how King Alfred, disguised as a minstrel, entered the Danish camp, in order to discover their plans. The Danes were so pleased with his performance that they wanted to keep him and it was only with great difficulty that he managed to escape.

Gradually Alfred managed to build up a fresh army, and a few months later (in 878) he marched out of his place of refuge, caught the Danes by surprise, defeated them at the battle of Eddington (in Wiltshire), pursued them back to their camp, and after a fortnight's siege, forced them to surrender. The Danish King Guthrum, who was in command of the Danish forces, and thirty of his leading followers were converted to Christianity, and baptized in King Alfred's presence. Treaties were signed whereby a frontier was drawn between Danish England (which came to be known as Danelaw), and Alfred's kingdom of Wessex.

Alfred was very well aware, however, that the peace was a precarious one. Accordingly he threw himself into the task of making his kingdom safe — and, he fervently hoped, of eventually expelling the Danes altogether from English soil. It was only too obvious that the main reason for the Danes' successes so far was the mobility conferred on them by their fast-moving warships, which enabled them time after time to achieve the element of surprise. Alfred determined to counter this advantage by building ships of his own. The interest he took in designing them was typical of his restless, inquiring mind. He revealed, too, that close yet imaginative attention to details which is the hallmark of the really great administrator. It is hardly surprising, in consequence, that King Alfred is often described as the "father" of the English Navy. He could also with some justice be described as the founder of the English Army. He completely reorganized the peasant *fyrd* or militia, so that it could be quickly and easily assembled when danger threatened, and he built a string of well-planned fortifications. He also took note of the Danish method of holding down conquered territory by the building of fortified towns, and rebuilt London as a walled and garrisoned town, held by English burghers, whose duty it was to defend it against attack.

Alfred's true greatness, however, lies in the fact that, harassed though he was throughout his reign by war or the threat of war, he never lost his vision of a stable, peaceful and civilized kingdom. He had a genuine passion for learning and culture, and assembled at his court (mostly held at Winchester, in Hampshire) learned men from many parts both of England and of Europe. There was nothing insular about Alfred's approach. He had been brought up to revere his European cultural heritage, and as a boy he had accompanied his father on a pilgrimage to Rome. He now re-established the monasteries as centres of religion and learning — and he himself translated various religious works from the Latin, to such good effect that he is often regarded as the initiator of English prose literature. Sir Frank Stenton, one of the most distinguished historians of the period, sums up King Alfred's achievements like this:

> His unique importance in the history of English letters comes from
> his conviction that a life without knowledge or reflection was un-
> worthy of respect, and his determination to bring the thought of the
> past within the range of his subjects' understanding.

In furtherance of this aim, Alfred established schools for laymen as well as for priests. It was he, too, who instituted the regular compilation of the *Anglo-Saxon Chronicle* (incorporating, as well, some of the earlier records) which was to continue long after his death and which is one of the main sources of information about the period.

His achievements in the sphere of government were just as remarkable. Always sensitive to regional as well as national sentiment and traditions, Alfred set up an administrative organization through the 'shires', or counties, and their various officers, which still substantially survives today. In addition, he borrowed from the Danes the organization of towns as semi-independent, part self-governing 'burghs', or boroughs, and this system too is still largely extant. There was, indeed, nothing either great or small to which he did not turn his mind. He took a great interest, for instance, in the designing of new types of houses; and he himself invented a highly efficient candle-clock.

His most remarkable achievement, though, was probably his compilation of a new code of laws, closely related in spirit and substance to the Bible, and selected from earlier laws, either written or traditional, including those not only of Wessex but of other Saxon kingdoms such as Mercia. Alfred has himself left a description of how he set about the task:

> Then I, King Alfred, collected these together and ordered to be written many of them which our forefathers observed, those which I liked; and many of those which I did not like, I rejected with the advice of my councillors, and ordered them to be differently observed. For I dared not presume to set in writing at all many of my own, because it was unknown to me what should please those who should come after us. But those which I found anywhere, which seemed to me most just . . . I collected therein, and omitted the others. Then I, Alfred, King of the West Saxons, showed these all to my councillors, and they then said they were all pleased to observe them.

It is obvious from this extract that Alfred went out of his way to stress that he had kept in close consultation with his councillors — another typical instance of his far-sighted statesmanship. The fact that he was careful to draw upon the laws of the other Anglo-Saxon kingdoms is also of particular significance. In doing so he was making it clear that although he was the King of the West Saxons, he felt a responsibility to all the English — including the English subjects of the Danish King Guthrum, whose interests he had carefully protected in the peace treaty.

Most remarkable of all is the humanity and liberalism of Alfred's approach in his Code of laws — as will be seen from these extracts:

> Judge thou very fairly. Do not judge one judgement for the rich and another for the poor; nor one for the more dear and another for the one more hateful . . .

> A man will not be the better because he had a well-born father, if he himself is nought. The only thing which is good in noble descent is this — that it makes men ashamed of being worse than their elders, and strive to do better than they . . .

Riches are better given than withheld. No man can have them without making his fellow men poorer. A good name is better than wealth. It opens the hollow of the heart; it pierces through hearts that are closed. It is not lessened as it goes from heart to heart among men. No sword can slay it, no rope can bind it.

It is hardly surprising that, when hard times came again after Alfred's death in 899 (at the age of fifty-one) the *Anglo-Saxon Chronicle* noted that "men longed for the laws of King Alfred". It is hardly surprising either, that the English revere Alfred the Great as the fountain-head of all that is best in British monarchy. He was one of the greatest warrior kings; but if he had never fought a battle in his life, Alfred would still rank among the great rulers of history.

5 Saxons, Danes -and Normans

ING ALFRED THE GREAT was not only great in his achievements, but also in his immediate descendants. In those perilous times, indeed, his work would have soon foundered if it had not been so. His gifted son, Edward the Elder, who reigned from 899 to 924, continued the process of gradually incorporating the Danelaw into his kingdom. His son Athelstan was equally able, and after he had gained victories over both the Welsh and the Scots, he styled himself, with some justification, King of all Britain. Athelstan's sovereignty, it is true, was still shadowy; all the same, it contained the first real premonitions of a monarchy of the 'united kingdom' of Great Britain.

In reoccupying the Danelaw these two kings ensured that many valuable aspects of Danish life entered permanently into the English system. The word 'law' itself is Danish in origin, and has outlasted both the Anglo-Saxon *doom* and the Latin *lex*. The Danes, in fact, when they weren't fighting, were fond of litigation and legal niceties. The principal officers in the towns of the Danelaw were often twelve hereditary 'lawmen', and the Danes also introduced the habit of making committees among the freemen at court. Some historians have seen in these practices a preparing of the ground for the future growth of the English jury system. Edward the Elder and Athelstan also took over and extended the Danish system of fortified boroughs (the names of many English towns still end in 'borough'—Peterborough and Middlesborough, for example) and combined with it the old Saxon division into shires.

Athelstan was succeeded by his two brothers—first Edmund (940–46)

The Danish Kings of England (1013–1066)

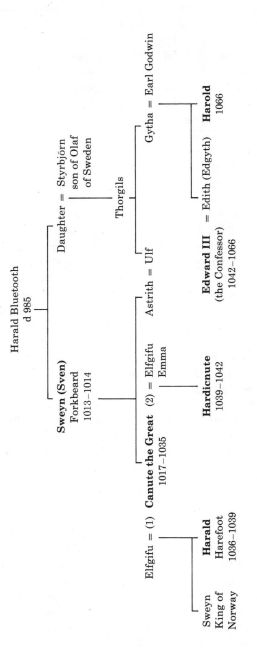

Harald Bluetooth
d 985

Sweyn (Sven)
Forkbeard
1013–1014

Daughter = Styrbjörn
son of Olaf
of Sweden

Thorgils

Elfgifu = (1) Canute the Great (2) = Elfgifu
1017–1035   Emma

Astrith = Ulf

Gytha = Earl Godwin

Sweyn
King of
Norway

Harald
Harefoot
1036–1039

Hardicnute
1039–1042

Edward III = Edith (Edgyth)
(the Confessor)
1042–1066

Harold
1066

and then Eadred (946–55). Both of them continued the process of extending and consolidating the kingdom of Wessex. Edmund — "the deed-doer", as the *Anglo-Saxon Chronicle* calls him — had a number of rebellions to contend with, but he eventually suppressed them. He seized further Danish territory, and defeated the Northumbrians and their Norwegian allies — and entrusted Strathclyde to Malcolm, King of Scotland, "on condition", according to the *Anglo-Saxon Chronicle*, "that he should be his fellow-worker by sea and land". When Edmund himself was killed by an outlaw, he was buried at Glastonbury Abbey in Somerset (an area associated with the legendary King Arthur), where the Abbot was the learned Dunstan (later Saint Dunstan), who had been one of Edmund's chief advisers. Dunstan was also friend and adviser to Eadred, who had in his turn to fight the Northumbrians (now ruled by a Norwegian king, Eric, colourfully known as Bloodaxe) before he took the whole kingdom of Northumbria under his own rule in the hope of preventing further trouble from that quarter.

In spite of all this warfare, therefore, when Eadred died the inheritance of Alfred the Great was not only intact, but enlarged and strengthened. It was just as well, because the next generation was represented by Edmund's two teenage sons. Eadwig, the elder of them, reigned only four years, and his brother Edgar was still only sixteen when he ascended the throne in 959. But so well established and stable was the kingdom of Wessex under the wise guidance of Dunstan (Archbishop of Canterbury after 961) that the *Anglo-Saxon Chronicle* was able to report of Edgar: "God granted him to live his days in peace." He had already, before Eadwig's death, ruled as king of Mercia and Northumbria (where he was preferred to his brother). So when he succeeded Eadwig, he too could with some justification claim to be king of a united England.

In 973 an event took place of profound significance for the future of the British monarchy. Edgar was now thirty — the age at which, in those days, a man could be ordained as a priest — and he decided to assert his kingship anew by having the Archbishop of Canterbury crown and anoint him in a solemn religious ceremony at Bath (in Somerset). The special importance of this ceremony was that it emphasized the analogies of kingship and priesthood, and provided for the first time in England a fully elaborated coronation service.

Not long after, another event took place which signalized Edgar's prestige and power. Eight kings, including those of Wales, Scotland and Strathclyde paid him homage at Chester. According to tradition the kings, as a symbol of their submission, rowed King Edgar in a boat on the Dee, a river near the Welsh border.

These outward appearances of stability and power were, however, in
many respects deceptive. The vassal kings paid lip-service only to the

suzerainty of the kings of Wessex. A latent danger, moreover, already existed in the early deaths of the Alfredian house, though hitherto it had been concealed by hereditary ability. But the danger was made only too apparent when Edgar's elder son, Edward the Martyr, was treacherously murdered in cold blood when a mere boy, in the interests of his ten-year-old half-brother Aethelred.

Aethelred's reign was a long one — from 978 to 1016 — but it was a disaster for England. He was the pawn of unworthy court favourites, and proved so lacking in wisdom and foresight himself that his subjects, in a bitter play on the meaning of his name (that is, 'noble counsel' — *rede* was the Anglo-Saxon for counsel), nicknamed him Aethelred the Unready — devoid, that is, of wise counsel. He was quite incapable, in fact, of dealing with the terrible new crisis that confronted his country. This was a renewal of the Viking onslaught, led by Sweyn Forkbeard, king of Denmark. It was directed against south-east England, for Sweyn did not attack the remaining parts of the Danelaw (just as he spared Normandy — the land of the Normans, or Norsemen, who had settled in northern France). At the same time, the part-Danish inhabitants of Yorkshire and East Anglia (which had once belonged to the Danelaw) did nothing to thwart the invaders or to help a now decadent Wessex. The only really effective resistance came from the citizens of London, the city which Alfred the Great had fortified a hundred years before and which now magnificently fulfilled the hopes he had placed in it. As for Aethelred, his only real strategy was to try to buy off the Danes by paying them huge sums of ransom, or *Dangeld* (that is, gold for the Danes). Eventually he was forced to flee to Normandy — he had earlier married Emma, daughter of Duke Richard of Normandy, thus making the earliest link between England and Normandy.

When King Sweyn died in 1014, Aethelred was able to return to the still defiant London, but died himself some two years later. There was a brief revival of Saxon fortunes under his son Edmund, whose nickname Ironside gives some idea of his redoubtable qualities. He fought a series of battles with Sweyn's son Canute (or Knut) for possession of Wessex (which had already submitted to Canute) at the end of which an uneasy peace left the kingdom divided between the two contenders. But Edmund Ironside's sudden death left the Witan with no alternative but to confer the crown on Canute.

As it turned out, England was fortunate. In many respects, Canute (who reigned from 1017 to 1035) was a king of whom Alfred himself might have approved, and he too earned the title of Great. For one thing, Canute the Great was a devout Christian (many of his fellow Danes and other Scandinavians were still pagans), and he entered into a close alliance with the English churchmen. In 1027 he secured many privileges   31 for English pilgrims to Rome, when he attended the coronation of the Holy Roman Emperor Conrad II, and found himself surrounded by the greatest princes of Europe — writing to England he reported that "they all received me with honour, and honoured me with lavish gifts".

Above all, Canute set out to heal the rift between Anglo-Saxon England and the Danelaw — so that in 1018 the *Anglo-Saxon Chronicle* was able to report:

> King Canute, with the advice of his counsellors, completely established peace and friendship between the Danes and the English, and put an end to all their former strife.

These counsellors, moreover, were Saxons as well as Danes. Canute took great care to preserve the old Saxon institutions. It is significant, for instance, that the *Anglo-Saxon Chronicle* also announced that the counsellors "determined that . . . they would ever . . . love King Canute with due loyalty — and zealously observe Edgar's laws". In other words, Canute allowed Edgar, the Saxon king, to emerge as the model of kingship, tactfully ignoring Aethelred and the period of anarchy and misgovernment which had intervened since Edgar's death. In addition he kept his unruly Danish nobles in check, dismissing a number of them and replacing them with Saxons. It was in this way that the Saxon Godwin was appointed to the earldom of Wessex, which Canute had created. Canute's wisdom and statesmanship, in fact, became proverbial — and gave rise to one of the most famous of English royal legends, according to which Canute — when his courtiers kept referring to his

---

Page 33: Prince Charles, wearing the robes of the Prince of Wales.

Page 34: The investiture of Prince Charles as Prince of Wales, at Caernarvon Castle, in 1969. After the Prince had been invested with the insignia of the Principality, he did homage to the Queen, his mother, declaring:
> "I, Charles, Prince of Wales, do become your liege man of life and limb and of earthly worship, and faith and truth I will bear unto you to live and die against all manner of folks."

Page 35: A photographic study of the Queen, Prince Philip, and their two youngest sons, Prince Andrew and Prince Edward, taken in 1975.

Page 36 above: The Queen attending the Braemar Gathering, at which games traditionally associated with the Highlands of Scotland take place.

Page 36 below: The Queen at a race meeting.

power in grossly flattering terms — had a throne put on the seashore, and sat in it ordering the incoming tide to retreat. As the sea naturally continued to advance, he turned to his courtiers saying, "Now you see that my power, like that of any other king, has its limitations!" The courtiers' awe of Canute is perhaps understandable in view of the fact that as king of Denmark and Norway, as well as England, he was certainly one of the most powerful monarchs of Europe, often referred to as an Emperor.

Canute's reign marked, in consequence, a constructive period in the history of the British monarchy. In view of his intention to rule as the successor to the kings of Wessex, it did not in effect imply any real break in the flow of English life, and it was probably in pursuance of this policy that he had married Aethelred's widow, Emma. Moreover, although he was succeeded by two incompetent sons who soon dissipated most of his work of reconciliation and unification, seven years after Canute the Great's death (in 1035) it was Edward, son of Emma and Aethelred, who ascended the throne and restored the old Saxon line.

Edward the Confessor, as he was known, was already nearly forty years old at his accession in 1042, and he had spent most of his life at the court of his cousin William, Duke of Normandy. Edward was an able man, but his chief concern was with religion and he had no real wish for temporal power. Much of his energy was devoted to the founding and upkeep of various religious institutions — and he also rebuilt Westminster Abbey, where the coronations of English kings and queens have been performed over the centuries.

From the beginning Edward surrounded himself with Norman advisers, and — far more important — it is highly likely that he promised his throne to his cousin William. The Saxon nobles resented this, and the most powerful of them, Godwin, Earl of Wessex, persuaded the King to marry his daughter Edith, though it is said that Edward deliberately refused to give her an heir. When Godwin died, his son Harold became the most influential man in the kingdom. In 1063, however, Harold had an extraordinary adventure. He was fishing in the English Channel when a gale blew his ship on to the French coast. He was captured by a French count, imprisoned and held to ransom. He was rescued by William of Normandy — but found that in order to be released he had to swear an oath to support his rescuer's claim to the English throne. According to tradition, Harold afterwards discovered that he had sworn the oath on some particularly sacred relics, though William had kept him in ignorance of this fact.

Nevertheless, when Edward the Confessor was dying he cancelled his earlier promise to William, and nominated Harold as his successor (perhaps under persuasion, perhaps because he feared the disruption of 37 his kingdom), and the Witan confirmed his choice. Harold had royal blood in his veins, through his mother, but there were other claimants more directly descended from Alfred the Great — and in this connection an important point about the Saxon monarchy must be made. Although the descent of the throne in Saxon times bore an hereditary aspect, there was no principle of primogeniture. In the tenth century, for instance, only three out of eight kings immediately succeeded their fathers. The death of each king was followed by an election by the Witan of the most suitable candidate. Royal blood was the prerequisite, but in many respects the monarchy at that time could be called an elected one. It was only after the Conquest that the right to succession by the first-born began to be established.

Although Harold was now king, William of Normandy was determined to follow through his own claim to the throne of England. He obtained the powerful support of the Pope, perhaps by making use of Harold's broken oath. He also encouraged Harold's disaffected brother Tostig to join forces with Harald Hardrada, King of Norway, in an invasion of the country from the north. Harold inflicted a tremendous defeat on the invaders at the battle of Stamford Bridge, near York. Both Tostig and Harald Hardrada were killed and so many of their soldiers that, whereas more than 300 ships had been needed to bring the Norwegians to England, only 25 were needed to take away the survivors. But a few days later, Harold learned that Duke William of Normandy had landed on the south coast. By forced marches he hurried back to confront him. The battle of Hastings was fought on Saturday, October 14th, 1066. It was in fact a battle on a much smaller scale than Stamford Bridge, and if only Harold had waited till his troops had rested and until he had collected reinforcements, he would almost certainly have won it. Even as it was, the battle was a very close thing. The Normans possessed one great military advantage in their heavily armed cavalry; but Harold countered this by placing his men on the crest of a hill, where their interlocked shields formed a wall against which the Norman horsemen hurled themselves in vain time after time.

When William saw that he could not take the English position by direct assault, he decided to try a ruse. He ordered his men to feign flight, and so lured the English from their hilltop in pursuit. The Normans then turned on their pursuers. Even now, though, the battle was not over. For three hours more the fight raged round the English royal standard, and once more the knights of Normandy were beaten back. Then William ordered his archers to shoot into the air, "that the arrows", the *Anglo-Saxon Chronicle* recorded, "might fall like bolts from heaven". Harold fell, pierced through the eye; the English faltered, and William had won the most important battle in the history of England.

The last of the Saxon kings had died a hero's death; his Norman conqueror marched into London where the Witan submitted and offered him the Crown. The coronation of William I took place on Christmas Day. A new chapter had begun for the English nation and the English monarchy. It is fitting that 1066 is the one date at least that every Englishman knows.

6 The Norman Kings

HE ENGLISH usually think of William I as William the Conqueror, partly because of the completeness of his conquest, and partly because he was to be the last foreign invader to set foot on English soil. William himself, however, was anxious to establish the legality of his claim to the English throne. He stressed his cousinship to Edward the Confessor, Edward's alleged promise to nominate him as his successor and the oath Harold had taken to support that nomination — and it was as the rightful heir to Edward that William had himself crowned.

It was in part to emphasize the legality of his accession that he gave orders for the weaving of the famous tapestry — which can still be seen at Bayeux, in northern France. At one time it was thought that it was woven just after the Conquest, and tradition attributed it to William's queen, Matilda. In fact it was almost certainly made in Kent about the year 1080. Its propagandist purpose, at any rate, is clear: it depicts from William's point of view the story of the Conquest and the events leading up to it, and it is in effect the first political strip cartoon in European history.

It was indeed in order to strengthen his claim to the English throne that William had married Matilda of Flanders in 1053 — for she traced her descent in the female line from Alfred the Great, and the marriage took place two years after the visit which William had made to Edward the Confessor, at which he had probably received Edward's promise to nominate him to the Witan as his successor. It was not only through Matilda, in fact, that the Saxon royal line survived in Britain. The saintly

40

The Norman and Plantagenet Kings of England (1066–1377)

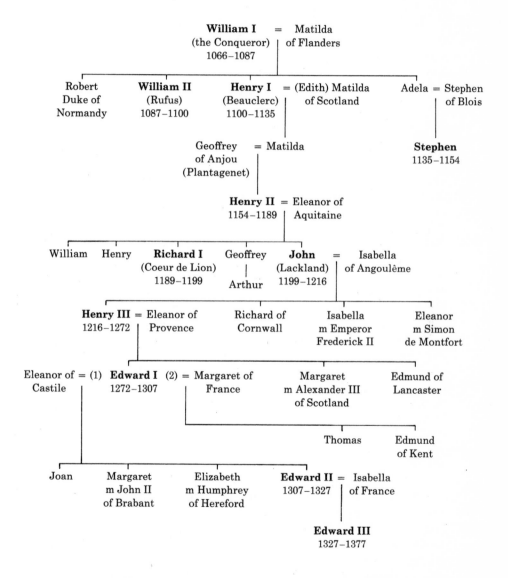

Margaret, Queen of Scotland, was descended from Alfred, Edgar and Aethelred; and William's fourth son (later Henry I) married another Matilda, who was the daughter of St Margaret of Scotland. In other words, the royal house of Alfred was preserved — and our present Queen has Saxon as well as Norman blood in her veins.

Anglo-Saxon resistance to William did not cease with the death of Harold, the last Saxon king. William suppressed the various risings with terrible ruthlessness — so that the *Anglo-Saxon Chronicle* (still being compiled by English monks at Peterborough) commented:

> Stark he was to men who withstood him; so harsh and cruel he was that none withstood his will; all men were obliged to be obedient, and to follow his will, if they would have lands or even life.

Even after William had devastated large areas (parts of Yorkshire, for instance, took nearly a century to recover) sporadic resistance continued. The leader of one of the guerilla bands, Hereward the Wake (that is, the ever-wakeful), is still regarded as one of the great legendary English heroes. He was a Saxon landowner near Peterborough in eastern England. He knew the Isle of Ely and the surrounding fen country intimately, and conducted a brilliant semi-amphibious warfare against the Normans. William had to mount a major campaign against him. After his final defeat Hereward disappears from history, but according to legend he escaped and continued to conduct raids against the Normans for many years, until eventually William granted him a royal pardon.

Neverthless the Conquest was in effect completed by 1072. It was consolidated by a large-scale confiscation of Saxon lands and by a network of keeps and castles. William also conducted a survey of his new kingdom, known as the Domesday Book. Its astonishing thoroughness can be gauged by this comment (still strongly Saxon in tone) in the *Anglo-Saxon Chronicle*:

> So narrowly did he cause the survey to be made that there was not one single hide nor rood of land, nor — it is shameful to tell but he thought it no shame to do — was there an ox, cow, or swine that was not set down in the writ.

The Domesday Book was compiled primarily for fiscal purposes, but also in order to hasten and institutionalize the transfer of the Saxon lands to William's Norman barons and knights. It was also tantamount to the imposition of the Norman brand of feudalism. Fundamental to the feudal system was the holding of land in fief (or fee) from the king (the overlord who in theory owned all the land) through a series of vassals, each of whom, in the ceremony of homage and fealty, undertook to serve his lord, who in return promised his protection. The barons who had thus sworn their loyalty to the king, in turn created lesser vassals, bound by the same oaths of fealty, to themselves.

The feudal system was common to most of Europe at the time, and had in fact already begun to establish itself in England under the Saxon kings. But there was a special feature about the kind of feudalism which had prevailed in William's dukedom of Normandy: William had imposed on his barons an authority far more complete than the rulers of the more strictly feudal countries could ever hope to wield. The Conqueror and his sons transplanted these Norman monarchical principles to English soil, where they reinforced the English kingship and developed it into a great medieval monarchy which had no parallel in any other country of Europe.

William further strengthened the monarchy by creating an efficient administrative machine, and by establishing a strong code of laws. Some of these were very harsh — particularly the game laws, for William was particularly fond of hunting: as one contemporary put it, "He loved the tall deer like a father." Nevertheless, by the time of William's death in 1087 England was a land where the rule of law prevailed — so that even the *Anglo-Saxon Chronicle* admitted:

> It is not to be forgotten that good peace he made in this land, so that a man might go over his kingdom with his bosom full of gold . . . and no man durst slay another.

There were many other positive achievements to his reign, including the establishment of good relations with the Church, and the building of cathedrals which are among England's greatest architectural treasures. By joining England to his great possessions in France, William the Conqueror had also turned England away from the Scandinavian influence, and in the direction of the Continent, with its more truly European political, religious and cultural heritage.

For a time after William's death it seemed as if the more positive results of the Conquest would be squandered. William's son, William II, or William Rufus, as he is commonly known (because of his red hair), though an able king in many ways, who secured the frontiers of his country by building Carlisle Castle on the Scottish border, and a chain of forts along the Welsh border, was cruel, avaricious and tyrannical. But when in 1100 he was killed by an arrow while hunting in the New Forest — the site of his death is still marked by the Rufus Stone — he was succeeded by his very able brother, Henry I — the youngest and only English-born son of the Conqueror — who came to be known both as Beauclerc, in deference to his learning, and also as The Lion of Justice. He issued a Charter of Liberties soon after his accession, in which he undertook to abolish the evil practices of William Rufus, created a new Royal Council, which more or less took the place of the old Saxon Witan, and again made royal justice a reality by sending his representatives all over the kingdom. He also made a point of calling upon the support of his English subjects against turbulent Normans. The most powerful of these was his brother Robert, who, although the eldest son of William the Conqueror, had been left not the crown of England but the dukedom of Normandy — partly because he had led a rebellion against his father. Henry was involved in constant conflict with Robert, until he invaded the badly governed dukedom, defeated him and held him prisoner in England for the remaining twenty-eight years of his life. To hold Normandy, though, Henry was obliged to wage nearly constant warfare — an ominous premonition of the blood and treasure to be poured out by later English kings in pursuance of their French territorial claims.

In 1120, Henry's only legitimate son, William, was drowned on his way from Normandy. To succeed him when he died (in 1135) Henry nominated his daughter Matilda (the widow of the German Emperor Henry V), who had taken Geoffrey, Count of Anjou, as her second husband. The Council, however, considering a woman unfit to rule, appointed Stephen of Blois, grandson of the Conqueror, to reign instead. What followed was known as "the nineteen long winters". Stephen was a weak and incompetent ruler. Although he won a battle against David, King of Scotland, when in 1138 the latter invaded the north of England on behalf of Matilda, Stephen had to cede the whole of Cumberland to him. Then three years later Matilda herself invaded and a civil war ensued which reduced the whole country to a state of anarchy, in which the barons cynically threw in their lot with first one contender then the other, and plundered and terrorized at will. It was a time, a contemporary chronicler wrote, when "Christ and his saints slept".

It was also a striking testimony to the importance of the personal element in the maintenance of the rule of law at this period. The machine of government was not yet strong enough to work without the presence of a king who knew his own mind and was determined to have his own way. Fortunately for England her next king was to be just such a person. The struggle between Stephen and Matilda (who had briefly held the throne, until the Londoners — disgusted by her cruelty and avarice — rose against her) was eventually resolved by a compromise. Stephen was to retain the throne, but on his death, Henry — Matilda's son by Geoffrey of Anjou — was to succeed him.

Henry II, who thus became king in 1154, was the first of fourteen Plantagenet kings, whose reigns stretched over more than 300 years. The name Plantagenet derived from the yellow broom flower (*planta genista* in Latin) which Henry's father, the Count of Anjou, wore in his helmet — and which was eventually embodied in the royal family arms.

For the sake of convenience these fourteen kings are divided into three related lines: the Angevins (after Geoffrey of Anjou), the Lancastrians (of the house of Lancaster) and the Yorkists (of the house of York). Henry II, therefore, is also the first Angevin king of England. He was, indeed, as much a French monarch as an English one, and a good deal of his time (the whole of the year 1156, for instance) was spent on the Continent securing his possessions there and suppressing various rebellions. But he was undoubtedly one of the most remarkable men ever to wear the English crown; brilliant in intellect; fascinating, volatile, and dangerous in temperament; and intensely human.

King Henry II was also a man of outstanding ability. He restored law and order, banished the foreign mercenaries, demolished the castles of rebellious barons, and powerfully reasserted the power of the Crown. He strengthened and extended the practice, begun by his grandfather Henry I, of despatching the King's justices round the kingdom, from which in course of time grew up the body of Common Law — the law, that is, common to the whole of England, a law above local practice, the corruption of local officials and the tyranny of local lords. It would be difficult to exaggerate the importance of the contribution which this development made to the eventual unification of England and to the growth of those legal principles upon which the liberties of modern Britain have been built. It was King Henry II, too, who was largely responsible for laying the foundations of the modern English jury system.

It is for his quarrel with Thomas à Becket, however, that Henry is chiefly remembered by most people (unfairly, in view of his great achievements). Thomas à Becket had been one of Henry's boon companions, and as the first of the English scholar kings since Alfred the Great, Henry valued his friend's learning and intellectual companionship. He made him his Chancellor, and later appointed him Archbishop of Canterbury, confident that he would further his aim of curtailing the inroads of the Church of Rome upon the royal authority. But as soon as he was appointed Becket turned into an ascetic and a devout son of the Church. He thwarted Henry's plans, and eventually after various partial reconciliations, and further disputes, Henry in a fit of fury cried out (as a contemporary report has it), "Of the cowards that eat my bread, is there none will rid me of this turbulent priest?" Four of Henry's knights, overhearing these hasty words, made their way to Canterbury, broke into the Cathedral and murdered Archbishop Becket.

Few events in medieval history shocked the conscience of Europe so profoundly — or cast such long shadows in the memories of succeeding generations. In 1172, two years after the murder, the Pope officially pronounced Becket a saint, and his tomb became a place of pilgrimage. Henry (who had himself been profoundly shocked) submitted to an act of penance, in order to effect some sort of reconciliation with Rome, whereby he walked barefoot through the streets of Canterbury and endured flogging from a number of bishops and from the monks of Canterbury Cathedral. In large part, no doubt, the penance was an act of political expediency. Afterwards, in fact, Henry quietly had his own way in the matter of Rome's interference in civil affairs, and his quarrel with Becket marked the beginning of the long struggle between the English monarchy and the Church of Rome that was to culminate, over three centuries later, in the English Reformation.

King Henry II's personal life was in many ways a tragic one. His first son died in childhood; the second, Prince Henry, whom the king had designated to succeed him, also died. In 1173, his two other sons, Prince John and Prince Richard, jealous of their brother and egged on by their ambitious mother, Queen Eleanor, rebelled against their father, aided by the Scottish king. Henry crushed this and a later rebellion, and Prince John, his father's favourite and apparently reconciled to him, was made King of Ireland (which had earlier been colonized by Norman-Welsh barons), only to be thrown out by his own rebellious subjects. Finally, in 1188, when Henry was fighting the French king, Prince Richard threw in his lot with his father's enemy. By the terms of the peace treaty that brought the war to an end, Henry granted an amnesty to Richard's followers — and the sight of Prince John's name among them as well was said to have broken Henry's heart, and to have brought about his death shortly afterwards.

Nothing, however, can detract from the value of Henry II's services to the English monarchy and nation. He bequeathed to the treacherous sons who succeeded him a system so strongly established that it was able to withstand the long absences of the one, and the tyrannical nature and practices of the other.

The later 7
Angevin Kings

I N THE POPULAR IMAGINATION, King Richard I (who succeeded his father in 1189) has always been endowed with a greater aura of glamour than almost any other British monarch. He was known as Richard the Lion-Hearted because of the heroism he displayed in the Third Crusade. The ostensible purpose of the Crusades was to free the Holy Land from the "infidel" Saracens—but although the Crusades were religious in impulse, they were also the first phase in the outward expansion of the restless and energetic races of the new Europe.

Richard set out for Palestine less than a year after his accession. On his way home from the victorious Crusade in 1192, he was captured by his enemy Leopold, Duke of Austria. Leopold handed his royal captive over to the Emperor Henry VI, who imprisoned him in a secret castle and demanded a heavy ransom. According to tradition, Richard's whereabouts were discovered by his faithful minstrel, Blondel, who wandered through Germany and Austria playing Richard's favourite tune on his harp beneath every castle he came to, until eventually he reached the right one, where Richard answered his signal and Blondel was able to tell Richard's regents in England where he was. Whatever the facts, the ransom was paid and Richard returned to his kingdom.

In spite of all the romance, though, Richard was by no means an effective king as far as England was concerned. He spent only ten months of his ten years' reign in England, regarding his kingdom solely as a source of revenue, first for his crusading venture, and then, for the long war he conducted for the rest of his life against King Philip of France. Indeed he is reputed to have said, "I would have sold London itself if I could have found a rich enough buyer."

During Richard's absences, England was ruled by capable royal deputies backed by the strong administrative machine bequeathed to them by Henry II. Richard's brother John made himself much hated, however, for his numerous injustices and tyrannies, as well as by his intrigues to seize the crown for himself — and this was in part responsible for the mystique surrounding Richard, because many people idealized him as a warrior king who would come to their rescue. It is in this role that Richard appears in many of the tales of Robin Hood, one of the most famous of all English legendary heroes. Robin Hood was the leader of a band of outlaws living in the forest, conducting numerous daring exploits against wicked barons and their underlings, and robbing the rich in order to help the poor. The legends spread over a century and more, but Robin Hood was undoubtedly modelled on a real person — and the French historian Augustin Thierry sees him as:

> the last of the Saxons — holding out against the Norman conquerors
> as late as the end of the twelfth century.

The people's fears about John were amply justified when, on the death of his brother Richard in 1199, he ascended the throne — to become a kind of archetype of the "wicked king". His wickedness, combined with his incompetence, led paradoxically enough to developments of tremendous importance for the future of England and the monarchy. To begin with King John lost the dukedom of Normandy to the king of France so that by 1205 only a fragment of the vast continental Angevin empire remained. In the long run this enforced insularity (though there were many more wars waged to regain the lost territory) was to foster the emergence of the English nation state. In the second place, John quarrelled with the Pope over his appointment of Stephen Langton as Archbishop of Canterbury. When the Pope placed his kingdom under an interdict, John retaliated by confiscating the property of the clergy who obeyed the interdict, and by banishing the bishops. When the Scottish king, William the Lion, joined his enemies, John displayed considerable energy, forcing William to pay homage to him; and he also put down a rebellion in Ireland and subdued Llewellyn, the prince of still independent Wales. In the meantime the Pope had excommunicated John, and in 1212 he issued a bull deposing him, and entrusted Philip, the king of France, with the implementation of the sentence. John, finding his position untenable, was forced to make abject submission to Rome, agreeing (in 1213) to hold his kingdom as a mere fief of the papacy, subject to a yearly tribute. A campaign which John launched in France the following year proved a costly failure, and added to his difficulties.

None of these events endeared him to his subjects, and neither did the extortionate levying of taxes which they involved, nor the general misgovernment of which John was guilty. A genuine party of opposition came into existence — and one of its main leaders was Archbishop Langton. The great significance of this movement was that it was the first time in English history that influential people, representing a variety of interests, had co-operated to make a national protest against bad government. Langton and the barons forced John to meet them on Runnymede, an island in the Thames (now one of the most famous national shrines). There John was made to sign a document known as the Magna Carta or the Great Charter. Some idea of what this document means to the English tradition can be gathered from this passage by the great Victorian historian J. R. Green:

> One copy of it still remains in the British Museum, injured by age and fire, but with the royal seal still hanging from the brown, shrivelled parchment. It is impossible to gaze without reverence on the earliest monument of English freedom which we can see with our own eyes and touch with our own hands, the Great Charter to which from age to age patriots have looked back as the basis of English liberty.

It was not that the Charter contained anything new, for most of its clauses were derived from the earlier legislation of Henry I and Henry II — but what *was* new was the formal confirmation in written form. As J. R. Green says:

> the Great Charter marks the transition from the age of traditional rights, preserved in the nation's memory . . . to the age of written legislation, of parliaments and statutes, which was soon to come.

The common people of England, of course, figured little in the proceedings, which were conducted entirely by the great prelates and barons. Nevertheless, principles which were eventually to be of universal significance were laid down, and one article in particular lies at the very basis of the British judicial system:

> No freeman shall be seized or imprisoned or dispossessed, or outlawed, or in any way brought to ruin: we will not go against any man, nor send against him, save by legal judgment of his peers or by the law of the land.

And another famous clause is:

> To no man will we sell, or deny, or delay, right or justice.

In fact, not long after signing the Magna Carta, John broke his word, this time with the backing of the Pope, who, seeing a threat to legally 49 constituted authority in the Charter, officially annulled it. Civil war broke out, and after John had achieved some initial successes, the barons summoned the French to their aid. A few months later, John died and was succeeded by a nine-year-old son, King Henry III. During his minority England was efficiently administered by a regency, but when he assumed power, Henry proved no more satisfactory a king than his father. He was a devout son of the Church, who modelled himself on Edward the Confessor, and he was perhaps the greatest of all patrons of medieval ecclesiastical architecture. During his reign Westminster Abbey was rebuilt (much as it is now) in the Early English style, while many of the earlier massive Norman cathedrals were remodelled, and the singularly beautiful cathedral at Salisbury built between 1220 and 1266. But by his subservience to the Pope and his encouragement of corrupt foreign churchmen, King Henry III alienated the English clergy (thereby further deepening antipapal feeling) as well as the more politically minded knights and a number of the barons. These found a leader in the King's brother-in-law, Simon de Montfort, Earl of Leicester. Civil war broke out in 1258 — but again it was productive of further momentous developments for the future of England and its monarchy.

In many respects it was a continuation of the struggle for the Magna Carta, which King Henry III kept setting aside. But there was a crucial difference. Whereas in the previous reign there had been only two parties to the dispute — King John on the one hand, and the great barons and prelates (supported by the people) on the other, now there was a third party, the "bachelors" or rising class of knights and gentry, already accustomed to local responsibility as coroners and jurymen, and resentful of the power of the great barons. During the reign of King Henry III the practice grew of summoning some of the knights of the shires (though not on a regular basis) to attend the still purely feudal assemblies of the great barons, as tenants-in-chief of the King, sitting with the other members of the *Curia Regis*, or King's Council. There was not the slightest intention in this of forming a new kind of assembly, and neither had the idea of election or representation crossed anybody's mind. It was simply that it seemed sensible to find out what the knights, with their growing economic power, were thinking; and it was convenient to do so by getting them together at some central point. As it happened, about this time the term *parliamentum* came to be applied to this assembly, though it was still meant to imply no more than its literal meaning of 'parley' or 'discussion'.

The truly revolutionary step took place after Simon de Montfort had defeated the King at the battle of Lewes (in Sussex) in 1264, and took his eldest son, Prince Edward, prisoner. For de Montfort — as a means of enforcing his terms — summoned the King to a *parliamentum* and called to it not only two knights from every shire, but also, for the first time, two burgesses from each of the chartered boroughs. De Montfort did so largely because he knew that most of the knights and burghers were his supporters, and the Westminster Parliament (as it came to be known) had little resemblance to parliament as it is known today. Nevertheless, Simon de Montfort was the first of England's ruling classes to realize that government could be helped and strengthened by bringing representatives of all the communities together and talking with them.

Simon de Montfort was defeated and killed by Prince Edward at the battle of Evesham (in Worcestershire) in 1265. But the Prince had been quick to see the value of de Montfort's innovations, and when he came to the throne in 1272, he called frequent assemblies, partly because he found them the most efficient method of raising money for his wars in Britain and on the European continent, but also because, in his great work of reforming and unifying the legal and administrative system, it was the best way of keeping in touch with the views and grievances of the growing middle classes in the towns and counties, and of winning their support (the serfs, as yet, had no say in such matters). King Edward I, in fact, has been aptly described as "the Father of the Mother of Parliaments". In 1295 he called together one such assembly, which became known as "The Model Parliament", and to which he summoned representatives from the nobility, the greater and lesser clergy, the knights of the shires, and the burgesses of the cities. This was a wider cross-section than ever before, and it can be seen as the first shadowy beginnings of a division into Lords and Commons.

Besides being a great statesman and law-maker, King Edward I was also one of the greatest soldier kings of England. Among his military achievements was the final subjugation of Wales, between 1277 and 1282, its annexation to the English Crown and the proclamation of Edward's eldest son as the Prince of Wales — the title of all male heirs to the throne from that time on. Scotland nearly suffered the same fate as Wales. In 1296 Edward marched north, forced the Scottish king to surrender his crown, and confiscated the Scottish coronation stone. Scotland was saved by the emergence of two great national heroes. The first of these, Sir William Wallace, after a number of notable victories against the English, was eventually defeated by Edward and executed in 1305, after which Edward prepared a new constitution for Scotland, dividing it into sheriffdoms and — another significant pointer to the future — arranging for representatives of the Scots to attend the English Parliaments. But the spirit of Wallace lived on in Robert Bruce, who had himself crowned King of Scotland in 1306 and kept up an incessant struggle against the English. Edward, though now old and infirm, 51 began preparations for another expedition against Scotland, but died in the following year.

Before his death, he charged his son, also named Edward, to carry his bones with the army until the Scots had been utterly subdued. Instead the new king had his father buried in Westminster Abbey, under a slab bearing the epitaph:

> *Eduardus primus, Scotorum malleus, hic est*
> (Here lies Edward the First, Hammer of the Scots)

King Edward II proved an unworthy son of a great father. His chief interest was in a succession of corrupt favourites. The first of these, Piers de Gaveston, was eventually seized by the nobles and executed in 1312. It was only then that the King tried to put into effect the promise he had made to his father to subdue Scotland. He invaded the country with a large army, to be disastrously defeated by Bruce at the battle of Bannockburn in 1314. Although Edward made a later attempt to invade Scotland, that too was unsuccessful and the independence of the northern kingdom was secure for a long time to come.

King Edward II's elevation of two new favourites, the Despensers (father and son), together with his arbitrary and ineffectual government, aroused the bitter opposition of the nobles, one of whom, named Mortimer, was engaged in a guilty liaison with the Queen (Isabella, the sister of the French king, Charles IV). In 1326 Isabella led an army of malcontents from France, the Despensers were taken prisoner and executed, and Edward himself was captured, forced to abdicate in favour of his son, and imprisoned in Berkeley Castle (in Gloucestershire) where he was brutally murdered the following year.

The new King was only fifteen and the country was in effect governed by his worthless mother and her equally worthless lover. But in 1330 Edward seized the reins of power, banished his mother, and put Mortimer to death. King Edward III had ambitions of following in the footsteps of his grandfather, the Hammer of the Scots, and he invaded Scotland on a number of occasions. He gained some brilliant victories, as the result of which one king of Scotland was held captive in London, where he died, and another was forced to make a secret agreement with Edward whereby, if he died without male issue, his throne would revert to the English king. Scotland, however, succeeded in retaining her independence.

It was during the reign of King Edward III that the Hundred Years' War between England and France began. The underlying reasons for the long struggle were economic, aimed at the recovery of the lost French territories for the English crown, and with them control of the wine trade centred on Bordeaux, and command of the Channel ports for the export of English wool to Flanders. But the struggle was also concerned with Edward's claim, through his mother Isabella, to the throne of France. The claim (which was in point of law a flimsy one) was marked by Edward's quartering of the lilies of France beside the leopards of England on his royal coat of arms — and in fact the English monarchy's claim to the French throne was not officially abandoned until 1802.

In 1340 the English fleet gained a great naval victory at the battle of Sluys, though at first Edward was not successful on land. Then in 1346 he again invaded France with his eldest son Edward, known as the Black Prince (perhaps because of the black armour he wore or perhaps, according to some chroniclers, because of his black Angevin temper). There followed some of the most famous victories in English military history. First there was the battle of Crécy, in 1346, followed by the capture, after a twelve-month siege, of Calais. Then in 1356 the Black Prince won an equally devastating victory at Poitiers. The age of the modern nation state had not yet arrived, but these great victories produced a marked resurgence of English pride, centred on the monarchy — even though by the time Edward III died in 1377, all that remained of his conquests in France were Calais and four other fortified towns, together with the coastal lands around them. The sense of national pride, moreover, was not confined to the barons and knights, because the chief reason for the victories had been the tremendous slaughter inflicted on the heavily armoured knights of France by the English bowmen — members of the submerged and still fundamentally Anglo-Saxon race of actual or former villeins or serfs.

There was another important factor during King Edward III's reign that also helped to further a sense of racial pride and solidarity. In 1362, the English language replaced Norman French as the official language of the law courts, and it became fashionable to speak and write "the King's English". This new King's English had absorbed many elements of Norman French, but it was basically the language of the Anglo-Saxons — and Professor Trevelyan writes:

> There is no more romantic episode in the history of man than this underground growth and unconscious self-preparation of the despised island *patois*, destined ere long to burst forth into sudden blaze, to be spoken in every quarter of the globe, and to produce a literature with which only that of ancient Hellas is comparable. It is symbolic of the fate of the English race itself after Hastings, fallen to rise nobler, trodden under foot only to be trodden into shape.

This emergence of an English national language, literature and consciousness was from the beginning closely associated with the monarchy.

There were, too, further legal and constitutional developments at 53 this time. The office of Justice of the Peace, for example, was created in 1360. The volume of statutes, indeed, had been increasing steadily for some time and Parliament met frequently to pass them — and also to vote supplies for the French wars. Parliament showed itself quite incapable, however, of coping with the problems caused by the Black Death, a terrible plague (probably bubonic) which killed at least half the population between 1348 and 1350. Inevitably this created a desperate shortage of labour. Before the Black Death the old feudal system had, in many respects, begun to decay, with an ever-increasing number of villeins obtaining their freedom. Obviously this was now against the interests of the landlords, and Parliament (which was still their preserve) passed legislation both to check further emancipation, and to keep down the earnings of the free labourers, who knew that in a free market they could now command high wages. Although attempts were also made to regulate prices, they were unsuccessful. A wave of unrest swept through both sections of the labouring classes.

This reached a peak during the reign of King Richard II (son of the Black Prince and grandson of Edward III), who came to the throne in 1377 at the age of ten. During his minority the country was ruled by his uncle, the Duke of Lancaster (one of Edward III's sons). John of Gaunt, as the Duke was usually known, was unpopular, and when in 1380 he imposed a Poll Tax (a method of taxing the poor to finance the still continuing war in France) a peasants' revolt broke out. In 1381 the rebels marched into London, and forced the young king and the government to take refuge in the Tower. A section of the rebels were then persuaded to return home by Richard himself, who promised to liberate the villeins and commute their personal feudal services (particularly labour on their lords' land) into money rent. The remaining rebels, under their leader Wat Tyler, burnt John of Gaunt's palace and broke into the Tower, where they killed the unpopular Archbishop of Canterbury. Again the young king met the rebels, and when during the conference the Lord Mayor of London struck down and killed Wat Tyler, Richard immediately rode amongst Tyler's followers and pacified them by promising to meet all their demands. The rebels, who had never identified the King with his government (to them he was a person apart, their natural leader, they idealistically supposed, against oppression and tyranny), accepted his assurances and dispersed.

In fact none of his promises was kept, and the revolt was put down with the utmost severity. Nevertheless the voice of the submerged mass of the people had made itself heard in no uncertain manner and that was a fact that could never again be entirely forgotten. Wise kings and queens in the future were to realize that the support of the masses was essential for the preservation of a strong monarchy.

After the Peasants' Revolt, John of Gaunt's influence was weakened. Another baronial faction seized power, but in 1389 Richard declared himself of age, and for the next eight years ruled with a considerable degree of success and moderation. But in spite of the courage he had shown in the presence of the rebels, and the fact that in 1385 he also invaded Scotland and burned Edinburgh, he was fundamentally weak and vain. After 1394, he showed every sign of wishing to rule as an absolutist monarch — and to do away with Parliament, which had now become an established part of the national life. In 1399 John of Gaunt died, and his son Henry Bolingbroke, now Duke of Lancaster, returned from French exile — and it was Parliament who deposed and imprisoned Richard and conferred the crown on Henry. Richard, who died (probably by murder) the following year, was the last of the Angevins; and with the accession of King Henry IV, a new era had opened in the history of the English monarchy.

8 Roses - Red, White and Tudor

ITH THE ACCESSION of King Henry IV in 1399, the English monarchy entered into a period of dynastic crisis which lasted over a century. The main reasons were the existence of the two great royal houses of York and Lancaster, springing from the younger sons of Edward III, and the circumstances attending the seizure of the throne by Henry. The official excuse had been, according to a contemporary source, "default of governance, and undoing of the good laws". But the real truth was that Henry was a great magnate who had taken advantage of discontent to seize the throne by force. The fact that the rightful king, Richard II, had been deposed and shortly after almost certainly murdered (perhaps with Henry's connivance), leaving behind him a number of claimants to the throne whose titles were stronger than Henry's, inevitably meant that despite his undoubted ability, Henry's reign was, in the words of William Shakespeare: "A scrambling and unquiet time."

Following Richard II's death, his half-brothers led a revolt on his behalf, and when he had stamped this out, Henry had Richard's body exhibited in London in order to dispel a rumour that he was still alive. Then the Welsh, under Owen Glendower, descendant of Llewellyn (the last independent Prince of Wales), rose against the English king, and in 1402 the Scots invaded Northumberland. They were defeated by the Duke of Northumberland and his son, the fiery and chivalrous Harry Percy, or "Hotspur" (portrayed so memorably in Shakespeare's play *Henry IV*, Part I). Shortly after, however, Hotspur entered into an alliance both with the defeated Scottish Earl Douglas and with

The Houses of Lancaster and York (1377–1485)

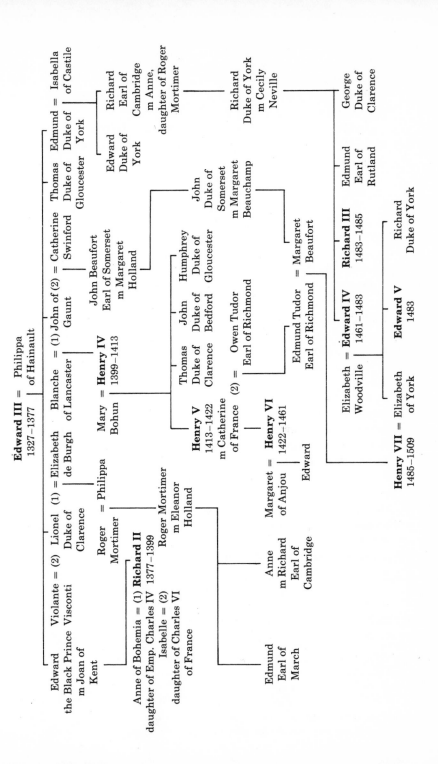

Owen Glendower, against Henry. They were defeated at the battle of Shrewsbury in 1403, Hotspur being killed and Douglas taken prisoner — though Owen Glendower continued the struggle, with the help of the French, until his death in 1416.

In the later years of his reign, however, Henry felt sufficiently secure to take advantage of the civil wars also raging in France, by sending two expeditions across the Channel. Nevertheless his kingdom was never completely pacified, and his difficulties were increased by the reluctance shown by Parliament in granting him the money he needed for his almost constant warfare — a symptom of the rapidly increasing concern of the Commons in financial matters. On the other hand, Henry dealt sharply with Parliament's proposal to confiscate the property of the Church, and encouraged the enactment of severe legislation against the Lollards, followers of the great religious reformer John Wycliffe (who had died in 1384). The Lollards, who had exercised a considerable influence on the Peasants' Revolt during the reign of Richard II, had already been condemned as heretics, but they were to continue to play their part in preparing the ground for the English Reformation and the eventual break with Rome.

During the reign of King Henry V, who succeeded his father in 1413, the dynastic crisis was in abeyance, and there was a nine-year interval of national glory and resurgence. In 1415 the young king laid claim to the French crown (through his great-grandfather, Edward III) and invaded France. In October of that year he won a famous victory at the battle of Agincourt against great odds, and largely because of his inspired leadership of the English archers, who cut down the heavily armoured French "as though they were hammering on an anvil", as a contemporary record puts it. So complete was King Henry V's victory that the French king was forced to give his daughter Catherine to him in marriage, and to recognize him as his heir in preference to his own eldest son, the Dauphin.

King Henry V soon became enshrined in tradition and legend as one of the greatest of all England's patriot kings. The kind of inspiration he provided later can be gauged from the famous exhortation which Henry addresses to his soldiers on the eve of the battle of Agincourt, in Shakespeare's play *Henry V*:

> . . . And you, good yeomen,
> Whose limbs were made in England, show us here
> The mettle of your pasture; let us swear
> That you are worth your breeding; which I doubt not;
> For there is none of you so mean and base,
> That hath not noble lustre in your eyes.
> I see you stand like greyhounds in the slips,

Straining upon the start. The game's afoot:
Follow your spirit, and upon this charge
Cry 'God for Harry, England, and Saint George!'

King Henry V died in 1422 of a camp-fever; if he had lived a few months longer he would (on the death of the French king) have been crowned in Paris as King of France. As it was his nine-month-old son (by his French Queen Catherine), also named Henry, assumed this title. But with the appearance in 1428, of the French heroine, Joan of Arc, English fortunes in France declined, the Dauphin assumed the throne of France, and when the war ended in 1453 Calais was all that remained of Henry V's conquests. Englishmen continued to mourn him as the ideal warrior king, cut off at the height of success and in the flower of his manhood. But it was his son, King Henry VI, saintly but subject to recurrent fits of insanity, who had to bear the brunt of the renewed dynastic crisis.

In 1454, when the King's mind was temporarily eclipsed, Richard Duke of York was appointed Protector by Parliament. On Henry's recovery, Richard, who was next in line to the throne, and whose claim was indeed much stronger than Henry's own, levied an army in order to maintain his power. The dynastic conflict had entered its most acute phase. It is usually known as the Wars of the Roses, because the house of York took as its emblem a white rose, and that of Lancaster (to which of course Henry VI himself belonged) a red rose. At the battle of St Albans in 1455, the Yorkists were victorious, and the King was taken prisoner. Shortly after he again fell ill, and Richard once more resumed his regency. When Henry recovered he did his best to reconcile the two factions, but St Albans was only the first of twelve ferocious battles between them.

In 1459 Margaret of Anjou, Henry's vigorous and capable Queen, rallied the King's supporters and in the following year the Lancastrians routed the Yorkists at Wakefield, and Richard was killed. In 1461, Edward the new Duke of York, with the help of his powerful ally Richard Neville, Earl of Warwick (known to history as "the King-maker"), defeated the Lancastrians and had himself proclaimed King Edward IV, later capturing Henry and imprisoning him in the Tower of London. Edward, however, quarrelled with Warwick, who entered into negotiations with Queen Margaret (now exiled in France) and the French King Louis XI. In 1470 Warwick led an invasion from France, deposed Edward IV, who fled to Burgundy, and restored Henry to a puppet's throne.

This was not the end of the merry-go-round, for, some six months later Edward returned from his exile, once more captured Henry, defeated the Lancastrians at the battle of Barnet, at which Warwick the King-maker was killed, and again at the battle of Tewksbury, at which Henry's

59

son was killed and Queen Margaret captured and imprisoned in the Tower (to be eventually ransomed by the French). On the same night that Edward returned to London from the battlefield, King Henry VI was murdered in the Tower (probably by Edward's brother, Richard Duke of Gloucester). So the Lancastrian cause had apparently ended in total failure, and the only positive achievements poor Henry, "the royal saint", had to show for his long and troubled reign was the foundation of Eton College and King's College, Cambridge.

The horrors attendant on the rivalry of the two royal houses were by no means over. King Edward IV exacted vengeance on his Lancastrian enemies and confiscated their estates. He also revived the old claim to the French crown and invaded France, but was bought off by Louis XI. He died suddenly in 1483, leaving behind him two sons, Edward and Richard, aged twelve and nine. The former, therefore, was now King Edward V, but his uncle, the hunchbacked Richard Duke of Gloucester, who had been appointed Protector, imprisoned both him and his brother in the Tower. After a number of plots hatched by the Lancastrians against the Duke, Parliament — now wanting above all else a really strong king — requested him to assume the crown. As Richard was a brave soldier and capable administrator, he might have fulfilled their expectations. But he blotted his reputation for ever by having his two young nephews murdered in the Tower, so secretly that the country did not learn of it till some time after. The story of the young Princes in the Tower has caught the imaginative pity of succeeding generations, and a melancholy footnote was added in 1674, when the skeletons of two children were discovered during alterations in the Tower of London. They were subsequently interred in Westminster Abbey and there they lie to this day.

Now at last, however, the long crisis of the English monarchy, and the ordeal of the English people, were nearly over. The Lancastrians had settled on Henry Tudor, Earl of Richmond, who was in exile in France, as their nominee. Henry was the grandson of Owen Tudor, a Welsh knight who had married Queen Catherine, widow of Henry V, and been created Earl of Richmond. His mother, Margaret Beaufort (the benefactress of St John's College, Cambridge), was the lineal representative of the house of Lancaster and a descendant of John of Gaunt by his mistress (and eventually wife) Catherine Swinford. His title to the throne was by no means a strong one, but it was as good as any other of the Lancastrian party. By now, indeed, most of the claimants, Yorkists and Lancastrians alike, had perished in battle or on the execution block. When Henry Tudor landed at Milford Haven, on the coast of his native Wales, he had only a small force with him. But the

Tudors were descendants of the ancient Princes of Wales, and Henry marched under the red dragon standard of Cadwaladr. His fellow-countrymen flocked to join him. Over the Welsh border he was joined by English sympathizers, outraged by Richard's murder of his two young nephews. The opposing armies eventually faced each other on Bosworth Field (near Market Bosworth in Leicestershire), and on August 22nd, 1485, the last important battle in the Wars of the Roses was fought. It was a decisive victory for Henry. King Richard III died, fighting bravely, and, according to legend, his crown was found some distance away from his body, caught on a thorn bush, from which it was removed and placed on the head of the victor.

The death of Richard III brought the ancient line of Plantagenet to an end and the accession of King Henry VII began a new dynasty and a new chapter in the history of the English monarchy and the English nation. In the following year the new king married Princess Elizabeth of York, daughter of Edward IV, thus finally merging the red rose of York and the white rose of Lancaster into the Tudor rose. One of the small curiosities of history is that when, during King Henry VII's reign, playing-cards were invented, it was a portrait of Elizabeth of York that was used for the Queens of the four suits, so that nearly five hundred years later her memory is still preserved with every deck of cards that is cut.

Not that this dynastic marriage immediately achieved the results Henry aimed at. The Yorkists were still strong in the North, and for a time they were in control in Ireland. In 1487 they put forward a youthful impostor, a baker's son named Lambert Simnel, claiming that he was the Duke of Clarence's son, Edward Earl of Warwick, who was in fact a prisoner in the Tower. The Yorkists had Lambert crowned in Ireland as King Edward VI, but when he and his followers landed in England Henry quickly crushed them. To Lambert Simnel himself Henry extended considerable clemency, granting him a pardon and—derisively perhaps—appointing him a servant in the royal kitchens (though he was also made one of the King's falconers). The real Earl of Warwick, however, he had executed, in order to remove at least one potential focus of rebellion. A more dangerous impostor was Perkin Warbeck, who in 1490 presented himself at the court of the Duchess of Burgundy, sister of Edward IV, as the younger of Edward's two sons who, it had been assumed, had met their deaths in the Tower. The Duchess professed to believe his story, as did King Charles VIII of France and King James IV of Scotland. With their backing Perkin landed in England in 1496, but eventually surrendered on the promise of a pardon. Henry kept his promise and imprisoned him in the Tower, but in the following year Perkin Warbeck escaped, and on his recapture was executed.

It was King Henry VII who fostered many of the developments which put England on the road to becoming a great power. He encouraged commerce and the material wealth of the country steadily increased. In 1496, it was he who was the moving spirit behind the sailing of John Cabot on the expedition which discovered Nova Scotia and Newfoundland. He granted substantial subsidies to shipbuilding and made a start on establishing a strong English navy. He exercised great influence throughout western Europe and he sought to ensure the future peace and prosperity of his country by two royal marriages. One was that of his eldest son Arthur to the Spanish Princess Catherine of Aragon. The outcome of this marriage was not in fact to be fortunate—because Arthur died and his brother Henry, when he ascended the throne in 1509, married his widow. But the other marriage, that of King Henry VII's daughter Margaret to King James IV of Scotland was eventually to bring about the union of the two kingdoms. It was an outstanding instance of the first Tudor monarch's statesmanship and far-sightedness —and his best epitaph perhaps is this—written over a hundred years after his death by the great Elizabethan and Jacobean writer and philosopher Sir Francis Bacon:

> This king, to speak of him in terms equal to his deserving, was one of the best sort of wonders: a wonder for wise men.

Father and Daughter 9
~ the great
Tudor Monarchy

ING HENRY VIII, who in 1509 ascended a throne more secure, thanks to the work of his father, than it had been for over a hundred years, figures chiefly in the popular imagination as "Bluff King Hal", the jovial but ruthless *bon viveur* who married six wives, and chopped off the heads of three of them. In fact he was a far more remarkable and complex character, involved in a far more complex situation, than this would suggest. He was one of the most brilliant of the princes produced by the European Renaissance and his accession was hailed with delight by such outstanding leaders of thought as Erasmus, Dean Colet, and Sir Thomas More.

His reign began with the happiest of auspices. He covered himself with glory, after he had invaded France, by winning the battle of the Spurs (so-called because the French knights, instead of "winning their spurs", fled ignominiously) and by capturing Terouenne and Tournay. The same good fortune attended him nearer home, for when the Scots took advantage of his absence and invaded England, they suffered one of the worst defeats in their history at the battle of Flodden. The aura of splendour was still bright when, six years later, Henry met the young King Francis I of France (who was looking for support in his quarrel with the Spanish Emperor Charles V) at an open-air conference so full of gorgeous pavilions, banners, and attire that it was known as the Field of the Cloth of Gold, and must have struck observers as an awe-inspiring blend of medieval chivalry and Renaissance magnificence. About this time the Venetian Ambassador to London wrote of Henry:

His Majesty is twenty-nine years old, and extremely handsome.

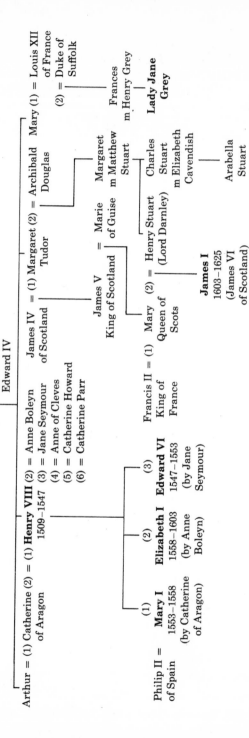

The House of Tudor (1485–1603)

Henry VII = Elizabeth
1485–1509   daughter of
Edward IV

Arthur = (1) Catherine (2) = (1) **Henry VIII** (2) = Anne Boleyn   James IV = (1) Margaret (2) = Archibald   Mary (1) = Louis XII
of Aragon   1509–1547 (3) = Jane Seymour   of Scotland   Tudor   Douglas   of France
                            (4) = Anne of Cleves   (2) = Duke of
                            (5) = Catherine Howard   Suffolk
                            (6) = Catherine Parr

James V = Marie   Margaret   Frances
King of Scotland of Guise   m Matthew   m Henry Grey
                                     Stuart

Francis II = (1) Mary (2) = Henry Stuart   Charles   **Lady Jane**
King of   Queen of   (Lord Darnley)   Stuart   **Grey**
France   Scots   m Elizabeth
                                             Cavendish

James I
1603–1625
(James VI
of Scotland)

Arabella
Stuart

Philip II =   (1)   (2)   (3)
of Spain   **Mary I**   **Elizabeth I**   **Edward VI**
                                                  1553–1558   1558–1603   1547–1553
                                                  (by Catherine   (by Anne   (by Jane
                                                  of Aragon)   Boleyn)   Seymour)

Nature could not have done more for him. He is much handsomer than any other sovereign of Christendom — very fair and his whole frame admirably proportioned. On hearing that Francis I wore a red beard, he allowed his own to grow: and as it is reddish, he has now a beard that looks like gold. He is very accomplished, a good musician, composes well, is a most capital horseman, a fine punster, speaks good French, Latin and Spanish, is very religious, hears three Masses daily when he hunts and sometimes five on other days.

To begin with, in fact, King Henry VIII was noted not only for his piety but also for his zealous championship of the Church of Rome. When in 1521, for instance, he published a book on the Sacraments — as a riposte, in terms of impeccable doctrinal orthodoxy, to Martin Luther, the German Protestant reformer — Pope Leo X conferred on Henry the title of "Defender of the Faith". He was now styled:

> By the Grace of God, King of England, France and Ireland; Defender of the Faith and in earth under God of the Church of England and Ireland; the Supreme Head and Sovereign of the Most Noble Order of the Garter.

The title of Defender of the Faith was borne by all his successors, and it can still be seen on all British coinage. He was, incidentally, the first English monarch to be called King of Ireland, after he had hanged the rebellious Earl of Kildare and five of his uncles — leading members of the Anglo-Norman aristocracy who had hitherto to all intents and purposes ruled Ireland. The Most Noble Order of the Garter, the premier (and very select) order of knighthood in England, had been founded about 1348 by Edward III.

But the central drama of King Henry VIII's reign began in 1527, when he sought a divorce from his Queen, Catherine of Aragon. Henry had fallen passionately in love with Anne Boleyn, a young woman at his court. The importance of this fact, however, has probably been exaggerated in the popular imagination. It was certainly not the only reason for Henry's desire to obtain a divorce. The only surviving child of his marriage to Queen Catherine was a daughter named Mary. A queen had never yet ascended the throne of England (apart from Matilda's brief and illegal occupancy) and Henry's desire for a male heir who would ensure an undisputed succession was quite genuine. The Wars of the Roses were still very much alive in men's minds, and the possibility that the battle of Bosworth might not have been permanently decisive was a nightmare that haunted both the King and his subjects. It was this fear, indeed (as well as Henry's personal popularity), that explains why the course of action he now pursued encountered so little really serious opposition in his own country.

65

King Henry VIII was certainly a man accustomed and determined to have his own way. His Chancellor, Cardinal Wolsey, said of him:

> He is a prince of royal courage, and hath a princely heart; but rather than miss any part of his will or pleasure, he will endanger the loss of one half of his realm.

Wolsey had been the King's right-hand man in implementing his policy of holding the balance between the rival powers of France and Spain (and thus increasing England's prestige and influence) and also in raising the necessary taxes to pay for that policy. Henry now entrusted him with the task of persuading the Pope to grant him a divorce from Queen Catherine, on the grounds that marriage to his brother's widow had been an unnatural union all along (and Henry really did appear to believe that the deaths of Catherine's other children in infancy, including the son born in 1511, were a divine judgement). Another factor in the case was that Wolsey believed that the time had come for a break with Spain, and a strengthening of the alliance with France by means (Wolsey hoped) of a marriage between Henry and a French princess.

At first the Pope seemed favourably disposed, but then, under strong pressure from the Spanish Emperor Charles V, he rejected Henry's petition for divorce. Furious with Wolsey's failure, Henry dismissed him in 1529. The next year he summoned him to face a charge of high treason, but Wolsey — a sick and broken man — died on his way to London. The gentle, learned and witty Sir Thomas More succeeded him as Chancellor until, realizing that the King was prepared to defy Rome no matter what it cost, he resigned in 1532. In the following year Henry secretly married Anne Boleyn — he wanted her as a queen who would bear him an heir, not as a mistress.

The final steps in the severance from Rome were now taken. A series of acts were passed by Parliament whereby the King's marriage to Catherine was declared invalid, and the Princess Mary illegitimate; the succession was vested in the issue of the King's marriage to Anne Boleyn; and the King was proclaimed as Protector and Supreme Head of the Church and Clergy of England. To this last act, Sir Thomas More — as a devout Catholic — was unable to swear, and he was executed in 1535. Further legislation provided for the dissolution of the English monasteries, partly on the grounds that they were potential hotbeds of dissension, partly on the grounds that they had become corrupt — and partly because, as Thomas Cromwell, the King's new Chief Minister, was quick to point out, the lands and possessions of the monastic orders furnished a lucrative source of revenue.

Although Henry's actions, and the religious and social revolution they entailed, were to a considerable extent dictated by personal motives, this was not the first time that the English monarchy had clashed with the claims of the Church of Rome to exercise jurisdiction over clerical and related matters in England. To some extent, therefore, the Reformation brought about by King Henry VIII was the culmination of a process which had been going on for a long time, and could be regarded as a necessary step in the achievement of England's absolute independence from foreign interference, and her emergence as a strong nation-state.

Certainly the removal of the Pope's authority in England had immeasurably increased the power and prestige of the Crown. Equally important for the future of the British monarchical system was the fact that the revolution, in its legal and constitutional aspects, had been accomplished by acts of Parliament. It was essential to the King that all the actions that he took in order to fulfil his underlying objective of obtaining an heir and securing the succession, should bear the stamp of legality — should, so to speak, be institutionalized. In achieving this, Parliament (which was increasingly coming to mean the House of Commons, because it was the lower House that held the purse-strings) was his obvious and natural ally. At the same time, Parliament itself benefited by thus being called to the forefront of affairs, and inevitably it gained valuable experience and prestige from the vast and momentous amount of legislation it was called upon to enact. The reign of King Henry VIII, therefore, saw a tremendous advance in that collaboration between monarchy and Parliament which was in the future to attend the most successful periods in English history.

Ironically, Queen Anne did not give her husband a son either — but another daughter, Elizabeth. Then in 1536 (the same year in which the ex-queen Catherine died) Anne was charged with infidelity and various other crimes, and subsequently beheaded, while Elizabeth, like her half-sister Mary before her, was declared illegitimate. Henry promptly married Jane Seymour, and a year later (in 1537) she died giving birth to the son and heir Henry had craved for so long. Henry had three other wives after that: Anne of Cleves, whom he married solely to further the Protestant alliance, and on condition that a divorce should follow speedily (Thomas Cromwell was beheaded for his part in arranging the marriage); Catherine Howard (a niece of the Catholic Duke of Norfolk), who was beheaded in 1542 on grounds of infidelity and treason; and finally Catherine Parr, who outlived him.

It was Jane Seymour's nine-year-old son, therefore, who in 1547 ascended the throne as King Edward VI. His uncle, Edward Seymour, Earl of Hertford, took over the Protectorship (and created himself Duke of Somerset). He encouraged the religious reformers and in 1549 his ally, Thomas Cranmer, the Archbishop of Canterbury, introduced his beautiful Book of Common Prayer, in order to secure uniformity of worship and, together with other steps, to carry the country farther along the road to Protestantism — though at the cost of provoking a rebellion of Catholics in Devon. There was also a rebellion of another sort, when Robert Kett, a Norfolk tanner, led a peasant rising. Both rebellions were suppressed in 1549. Previously, in 1547, Somerset had also successfully invaded Scotland, to try to enforce a marriage-contract (which in fact came to nothing) between King Edward VI and Mary, Queen of Scots.

Early in 1552, however, Somerset — accused of over-ambition by powerful members of the King's Council — was beheaded, and John Dudley, Earl of Warwick, took his place as Protector, also being created Duke of Northumberland. Besides being a far worse ruler than Somerset he was equally ambitious. In the hope of securing the succession for his own family, he married one of his sons to Lady Jane Grey, the daughter of the Duke of Suffolk, a distant heir to the throne and a staunch Protestant. Dudley then persuaded the boy-king, who was on his death-bed, to sign a will excluding both of Henry VIII's daughters, Mary and Elizabeth, from the succession and naming Lady Jane Grey as his successor. Three days after Edward's death (on July 6th, 1553) Dudley had Jane proclaimed Queen. But the hated Protector's plot, lacking any kind of popular support, quickly collapsed. The nation wanted the Tudor line to continue, and Mary, the Roman Catholic daughter of Catherine of Aragon, entered London in triumph. Lady Jane Grey was imprisoned in the Tower and John Dudley, Duke of Northumberland, was executed.

Queen Mary was determined to bring back Roman Catholicism. At first she proceeded cautiously, reinstating the Catholic bishops and imprisoning some of the leading Protestant reformers; but she dared not at this stage set aside her father's Act of Supremacy by restoring the authority of the Pope. The crisis of her reign came when she announced her intention of marrying her cousin, Philip, heir to the Spanish throne, although the House of Commons (realizing that such a match would threaten the future independence of the country) begged her not to do

Page 69: King John (reigned 1199–1216). In 1215, at Runnymede, he granted the Magna Carta — the famous charter of liberties which marked the beginning of democracy in England.

Page 70: King Richard III (reigned 1483–1485). He was the last of the Plantagenet kings who ruled England for over 300 years.

Page 71: King Henry VIII (reigned 1509–1547). He created the national church and established the Reformation in England.

Page 72: Queen Elizabeth I (reigned 1558–1603). Her reign was one of the most glorious periods in English history.

JOHANNES REX

so. The unpopularity of the proposal immediately led to a rebellion, led by Sir Thomas Wyatt together with Lady Jane Grey's father, the Duke of Suffolk. The insurrection was quelled largely through the courage and coolness of Mary herself. Lady Jane Grey, as well as her husband and her father were now executed, and in 1554 Mary married Philip. He remained in England over a year, and when in 1556 he became King of Spain and all her vast dominions, England had to all intents and purposes become the vassal of a foreign power.

Mary's next step was the passing through Parliament of an act restoring the full authority of the Pope in all matters of faith and spiritual jurisdiction — though the confiscated lands of the dissolved monasteries were not restored, and all that the rising new aristocracy (which had grown fat on the spoils) had to do to keep them was to pay lip-service to the old religion. The old heresy laws were also revived, and Mary devoted herself with fanatical zeal to the reconversion of the country — by burning at the stake some three hundred men and women, including Bishops Latimer and Ridley, and Archbishop Cranmer. All that the persecution in fact achieved was a strengthening of the Protestant faith in England, a fierce hatred of the Spaniards (though even they had, as a matter of policy, advised Mary against the burnings), and a no less fierce hatred of the Queen herself, who now became known as Bloody Queen Mary. To add to her unpopularity, Calais, which had been an English possession since 1347, was lost to France in 1558. When she heard the news Mary is said to have declared, "When I die the word Calais will be found engraved on my heart." Deserted by her husband, who had returned to Spain, Mary died shortly after, a lonely, embittered and childless woman.

The accession of her half-sister Elizabeth was hailed with joy and relief, not only by Protestants but by many patriotic Catholics as well. Their confidence was well placed because Queen Elizabeth I — Gloriana, as she came to be called by her adoring subjects — proved to be one of the greatest monarchs ever to occupy the throne of England. In many ways she was very much her father's daughter. As the contemporary portraits of her show, her hair was the same red-gold colour as Henry VIII's, and she had his shrewd blue eyes. She had a pale oval face and she was particularly proud of her delicate, long white hands. She took after her father, too, in intellect and accomplishments. When the Spanish Ambassador attended her court in 1564, for instance, he described how he found her listening intently to a "keyed instrument". She spoke to him first in Italian; he answered in Latin as he handed her his letter of credence; she read it, then replied to the Ambassador in Latin with, he reported, "elegance, facility, and ease". She also spoke other languages; she was an expert performer on the virginals; she was a patroness of the 73 arts, wrote poetry herself, and was the inspiration of the poets of the period — this was, of course, the age of Shakespeare, the greatest dramatic poet in the history of English literature.

At the same time, she was also her mother's daughter, and she made use of all her feminine wiles to play off the various enemies of the nation against one another and, exploiting her unmarried state for political ends, by pretending to favour first one then another suitor from the various royal houses of Europe. "This woman is possessed of a hundred thousand devils," one of the Spanish envoys protested; for to begin with the most persistent of Elizabeth's suitors was her half-sister's widower, King Philip II of Spain. Philip still hoped to bring England under Spain's domination, and back into the fold of the Roman Catholic Church. There was a complication in that France, the other leading European Catholic power, was Spain's greatest political rival — and Elizabeth's cousin, Mary Queen of Scots, who was the nearest heir to the English throne, was married to the Dauphin of France (who later became King Francis II). It was, therefore, in Philip's interests, at this stage of the game, to lend his support to Elizabeth against France, and against her cousin's pretensions to the English throne. It was the kind of situation she could be counted on to exploit to the full, with the help of her astute Secretary of State, Sir William Cecil (later Lord Burleigh).

In fact Elizabeth never married. It is likely that she knew she was barren, and she certainly had no intention of handing over her kingdom to a foreign husband. Of several royal favourites, the one she loved best and longest was probably the Earl of Leicester, who achieved a position of considerable authority until his death in 1588. But she was almost certainly aware that Leicester intrigued with both Protestant and Catholic powers for support in connection with his ambitions of obtaining the Crown for himself, and she had no intention of marrying him either. The real love of her life was England itself, and she was speaking the plain truth when, addressing the first Parliament of her reign, she said:

> Nothing, no worldly thing under the sun, is so dear to me as the love and goodwill of my subjects.

When she came to the throne she knew that her first tasks were to heal the wounds of the nation caused by the religious persecutions of her half-sister, Queen Mary, and to allow the country to grow strong again by a policy of peace and stringent economy. She knew, too, that her part in Europe must be that of a Protestant sovereign, especially because Pope Paul IV held that as, in the eyes of the Church of Rome, she was illegitimate, she must resign the Crown to him to dispose of as he thought fit, and further that England was merely a fief of the Holy See — an attitude which was increasingly to mean that for England Protestantism and patriotism were to a large extent synonymous. The Reformation initiated by Henry VIII was therefore continued by establishing the Church of England, with the sovereign as Supreme Head, in a form which is substantially the same today. As far as the new order of worship was concerned, the settlement was fundamentally a moderate one, a compromise between Roman Catholicism and the more extreme forms of Protestantism. But it was utterly repugnant (as, of course, was the settlement as a whole) to the adherents of the old faith (and later in Elizabeth's reign also to the extreme Protestants, or Puritans) and the Queen was forced, as a matter of political necessity, to take harsh measures against many Roman Catholics (as she did later against the Puritans). On the whole, though, she disliked such measures, and— writing some centuries later, the historian J. R. Green was right when he declared that Elizabeth was:

> the first English ruler who felt the charge of religious persecution to
> be a stigma on her rule; the first who distinctly disclaimed religious
> differences as a ground for putting men to death.

At the same time Elizabeth, while still taking care not to alienate Philip completely, helped the Protestant cause in Europe. The help was mostly undercover, as with that given to the Huguenots (or Protestants) of France at the time of the massacre of St Bartholomew in 1572, when thousands of them were put to death by the French king, with whom Elizabeth was temporarily in alliance. At other times the help was open, as when she sent an army, under the Earl of Leicester, to support the Protestants of the Netherlands who were in revolt against their Spanish masters—and Sir Philip Sidney, one of the most brilliant and accomplished of the Elizabethan courtiers and poets, died a hero's death at the battle of Zutphen in 1586.

The chief danger point for Elizabeth was the presence of the Roman Catholic Mary Queen of Scots, who in 1568 threw herself on Elizabeth's mercy after the Scottish Protestants had deposed and expelled her. Although Elizabeth kept her under close supervision, frequently changing her place of residence, for eighteen years Mary was a focus of intrigue (both foreign and domestic) aimed at the overthrow of Elizabeth, her replacement by Mary, and the restoration of Catholicism. There were several plots centred on the captive queen, especially after a number of Jesuits were secretly despatched to England to establish contact with disaffected English Roman Catholics. After the discovery of the most serious of these conspiracies in 1586, Elizabeth's ministers demanded the permanent removal of the threat. Elizabeth hesitated for a long time, but eventually she yielded, and Mary Queen of Scots was executed in 1587.

The great crisis of Elizabeth's reign now approached. Philip of Spain, 75 whose patience had been exhausted, vowed vengeance for the execution of a Catholic queen. But there were other more weighty considerations. He could no longer tolerate the help given by Elizabeth to his rebellious subjects in the Netherlands, and even more important, he could no longer put up with the attacks — by such English sea-captains as Sir Francis Drake (the first man to circumnavigate the globe) — on the treasure-ships coming from the new Spanish Empire in South America, rapidly becoming the corner-stone of the Spanish economy. These attacks were semi-piratical, but Philip was well aware that Elizabeth connived at them. It was Sir Francis Drake who, when news reached England in 1587 that Philip was planning to invade the country, sailed into Cadiz harbour at the head of an English squadron and set fire to the Spanish ships assembled there — an exploit which came to be known popularly as "the singeing of the King of Spain's beard".

In 1588, however, Philip's Invincible Armada set sail from the Tagus in Portugal (which was then under the Spanish crown), with 8,000 sailors and 20,000 soldiers, while a land army of 100,000 men stood by to be transported from the Netherlands. In England patriotic fervour (among loyal Catholics as well as Protestants) rose to fever-pitch. Elizabeth, as she so often did, found the right words to fit the occasion, when she addressed her troops assembled at Tilbury:

> We have been persuaded by some that are careful of our safety, to take heed how we commit ourselves to armed multitudes for fear of treachery; but I do assure you, I do not desire to live to distrust my faithful and loving people . . . and therefore I am come amongst you as you see at this time, not for my recreation and disport, but being resolved, in the midst and heat of the battle, to live or die amongst you all: to lay down for my God, and for my kingdoms, and for my people, my honour and my blood even in the dust. I know I have the body of a weak, feeble woman, but I have the heart and stomach of a king, and of a King of England too; and think foul scorn that . . . Spain, or any prince of Europe, should dare to invade the borders of my realm . . .

Her confidence was not misplaced. The English fleet, led by such re-doubtable captains as Lord Howard of Effingham, Sir John Hawkins, Sir Martin Frobisher — and, of course, Sir Francis Drake — inflicted a tremendous defeat on the Spanish Armada in the English Channel. The surviving Spanish ships were scattered by a tempest, and Elizabeth had a commemorative medal struck, inscribed with the words: "God blew his wind and they were scattered." This victory (of July 1588) marked a climax in the history of England as well as in the reign of Elizabeth. Largely owing to her efforts, England had escaped from her enemies 76 and emerged more powerful and united than ever before.

The closing years of Elizabeth's reign were embittered by the loss of her beauty, the treachery and faithlessness of one of her young favourites, the Earl of Essex, who paid the forfeit on the executioner's block in 1601, and by increasing loneliness and exhaustion. And almost exactly two years later, the diarist John Manningham made this entry:

> This morning about three at clock Her Majesty departed this life, mildly like a lamb, easily like a ripe apple from the tree.

But the last years did not dim the glow, and it was as Gloriana, the embodiment of all the aspirations of the English people, and the inspiration of the most brilliant period in English culture, that Elizabeth was to be remembered.

10 The Stuarts -King versus Parliament

QUEEN ELIZABETH I died early on the morning of Thursday, March 24th, 1603. As soon as the news reached them her ministers (chief of whom was Sir Robert Cecil, the second son of Elizabeth's great Secretary of State, Lord Burleigh) met to deliberate. At ten o'clock the same night a courtier named Sir Robert Carey, who had been standing by booted and spurred, mounted horse and rode north. By constantly changing his mount at the various post-stations, he made record progress and in spite of being slowed down towards the end of his journey by a bad fall, he reached Edinburgh on the Saturday night, was admitted to the presence of King James VI of Scotland — and hailed him as King James I of England. It was thus that Henry VII's far-sighted policy of marrying his daughter Margaret to James IV of Scotland in 1503 was finally vindicated. The new English king, Henry VII's great-great-grandson (and son of Mary Queen of Scots by her second husband and cousin, Lord Darnley), was — in view of the fact that Elizabeth had never borne children — the undisputed heir to the English throne, and thus the first of the Stuart monarchs to occupy it.

This union of the two crowns (though it was to be a long time before the two countries were to be administratively united and to share the same Parliament) was obviously a potential blessing of inestimable importance. King James I's reign, in fact, began under the most favourable auspices. For years Englishmen had been haunted by the question "What will happen when the Queen dies?" — and they were full of gratitude for the smooth transition from one reign to another. Nevertheless the year 1603 marks the beginning of the central crisis in the history of

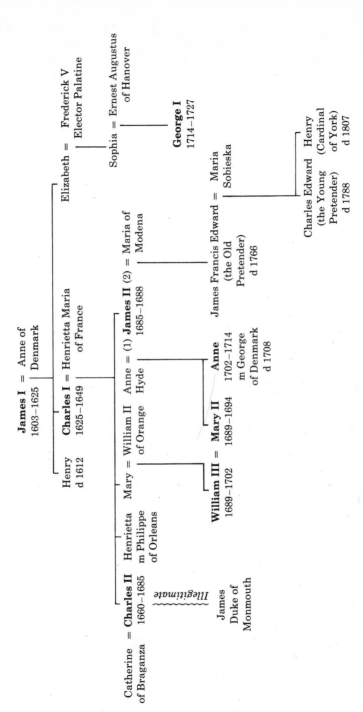

The House of Stuart (1603–1714)

the modern British monarchy. For it was during the first half of the seventeenth century that the crucial issue was decided as to whether the government of England was to be by King and Parliament, or, as in most other European countries, by King alone.

King James I's popularity did not last long. Unfortunately he was, in the words of the great nineteenth-century historian Lord Macaulay:

> made up of two men — a witty, well-read scholar who wrote, disputed and harangued, and a nervous drivelling idiot who acted.·

Or, as his French contemporary the Duc de Sully succinctly put it, James was "the wisest fool in Christendom". His new subjects were soon disillusioned. For one thing they resented the King's partiality for incompetent and spendthrift favourites. But what was far more serious was King James I's inability to understand the peculiar network of laws, traditions and customs that had brought the English Parliament into being. He made this only too evident when he declared:

> I am surprised that my ancestors should ever have permitted such an institution to come into existence. I am a stranger and found it here when I arrived, so that I am obliged to put up with what I cannot get rid of.

Such an attitude could hardly be expected to make for good relations between the King and Parliament. Neither did King James I properly understand the nature of the English monarchy, as it had evolved under his predecessors. The Tudor monarchs had all been powerful heads of state, but they had not been despots as many European (and most Oriental) rulers were. Indeed, without a standing army or a paid bureaucracy they could not impose their will upon their subjects by force. Theirs had to be rule by consent. It had succeeded to a large extent because of the political acumen of the two Henrys and Elizabeth, and even more because there was a hunger for strong government after the disastrous and bloody civil conflicts of the past, and because, at a less conscious level, there was a need for strong national leadership to ease the transition from the medieval to the modern world. In the process the Tudors had certainly inspired awe and devotion. But the basis of English king-worship was a matter of emotion not of doctrine. When, therefore, King James I in his pedantic way set out to turn this kind of king-worship into the political dogma of "the Divine Right of Kings", he was in fact destroying its essence. Ironically enough, he also cheapened the prestige of the monarchy when he degraded the royal prerogative of conferring titles, by virtually putting them up for sale.

His reign, however, did witness at least one positive achievement in
80 the religious life of the nation — the publication in 1611 of the Authorized

Version of the Bible, which was indeed a landmark in the literature of the country as well as in its religion. James's handling of ecclesiastical affairs, though, was for the most part clumsy and inept. His greatest blunder was his refusal to countenance any relaxation in the Church settlement of Elizabeth I that might have accommodated the Puritans, who were becoming increasingly powerful in trade and commerce — and also in Parliament. After an abortive ecclesiastical conference, three hundred Puritan clergymen were ejected from their livings. This marked the real beginning of English Nonconformity — refusal, that is, to conform to all the tenets of the established Church of England. In his fury against the religious dissidents, James declared: "I shall make them conform themselves or I will harry them out of the country." He was as good as his word: a number went into exile, and in 1620 a group of them, known as the Pilgrim Fathers, set sail for America in their little ship *The Mayflower*, in order to found a community in the New World where they could practise their religion free from interference or persecution. The foundations of a British empire beyond the seas had thus been laid, and in the course of time a great new nation was to emerge as the United States of America.

At the same time King James I was equally unsuccessful in dealing with his still numerous Roman Catholic subjects. He made promises of some mitigation of the legislation directed against them, which he was quite unable to fulfil because of his hostile relations with the Puritans in their now powerful position in Parliament, and also because of the fears of the nation as a whole of a revival of Catholic influence, at a time when the policy of the Papacy was still directed to the overthrow of the English Protestant Church and State. It was because of James's broken promises that in 1605 a group of Roman Catholics hatched the most famous plot in English history, in which Guy Fawkes and a band of conspirators tried unsuccessfully to blow up the houses of Parliament at a time when the King was there for the ceremonial opening of a new session. This event is still celebrated every November 5th with bonfires, fireworks and the burning of a 'guy' — an effigy supposed to represent Guy Fawkes (though it is doubtful if many of the participants know anything about its origins). A significant point about the plot, perhaps, is that whereas in earlier ages it was only necessary to murder a king in order to change the government, now the plotters felt it essential to remove Parliament as well.

In spite of all this, King James I initiated a highly unpopular policy of alliance with Catholic Spain, to cement which he sought to marry his son Charles to a Spanish princess. It was a match which, the English people clearly saw, might lead to Spanish heirs and Catholic kings who would endeavour to undo the work of Elizabeth I. In the process James further 81 outraged English patriotic feeling, which had been high ever since the defeat of the Spanish Armada, by allowing English sea-power to decline. The Navy fell into decay. Its proud claim that its flag must be saluted by ships of other nations sailing in English waters was abandoned. Pirates operated in the English Channel with impunity. The treaty by which James brought war with Spain to an end ignored the claims established by the Elizabethan seamen to trade with Spanish America and the regions monopolized by Portugal in Africa and Asia.

The greatest of the surviving Elizabethan seamen was Sir Walter Raleigh, brilliant poet, scholar and courtier; a one-time favourite of Elizabeth I, in whose name he had taken possession of Virginia in North America; and organizer of many expeditions against the Spaniards in Europe and the New World. On his accession James had imprisoned Raleigh in the Tower of London on a flimsy charge of treason. He released him in 1616 to lead his second expedition to the Orinoco (his first had been in 1595) in search of its fabled gold. The expedition turned out disastrously, and in the course of it, while Raleigh himself was ill, his men attacked a Spanish settlement. On Raleigh's return and at Spain's insistence, King James I ordered his execution. It was an action that roused the indignation of the English people; to them it seemed to symbolize the last brutal severing of the link with the proud past of Elizabeth's reign. The Spanish match was in fact ultimately abandoned, partly because of the bungling of James's current favourite, George Villiers, whom he had created Duke of Buckingham, and war with Spain followed. But the marriage of Prince Charles to another Catholic princess, Henrietta Maria of France (also negotiated by Buckingham), was no less unpopular.

The reign of King Charles I, who came to the throne on the death of his father in 1625, began, therefore, under the most unfavourable circumstances, especially as the hated Duke of Buckingham retained his ascendancy. He initiated various military and naval expeditions, including one against Cadiz in Spain, which proved to be costly fiascos which further lowered the prestige of nation and monarchy alike. Assassination removed Buckingham from the scene in 1628, but unfortunately King Charles I, although he was brave, cultured and accomplished, had inherited his father's poor judgement, unbending nature and tactlessness. His marriage was a happy one, but he allowed his Roman Catholic queen to exert an influence on affairs which was greatly resented by his Protestant subjects. In particular, he could no more tolerate the claims of Parliament than his father had done. In order to get money to pay for his disastrous wars with both France and Spain (brought to an end in 1629 and 1630), he was forced to grant the Petition of Rights, which confirmed the privileges of Parliament, and
has been compared with Magna Carta in its theoretical implications.

But it did not prevent Charles from dissolving three Parliaments in the first four years of his reign. In addition, he ignored one of the House of Commons' most treasured privileges — that of freedom from arrest for its members (a privilege which had always been respected by Elizabeth I) — by throwing three members of Parliament into prison, where one of them — Sir John Eliot — died, thus becoming a martyr to the Parliamentary cause.

After 1629 Charles ruled for eleven years without a parliament. But by thus attempting to rule by despotic means, he came into collision with the English Common Law, still the enemy of absolute royal power and the great ally of Parliament, and in particular with a redoubtable lawyer, and friend of Sir John Eliot, named Sir Edward Coke. The King, following in his father's footsteps, argued according to Roman Law, that the will of the monarch was itself the source of law, and that the judges were merely "lions under the throne", bound to speak as the monarch directed them. Coke, on the other hand, in the spirit of the English Common Law, conceived of law as having an independent existence of its own, set above the king as well as above his subjects, and bound to judge impartially between them. The laws were alterable only in the highest court in the land — the High Court of Parliament. In many respects the battle between the King and Parliament was really the battle between these two principles.

In carrying out his policy, King Charles was assisted by two men, each great in his own way, but each largely instrumental in bringing about the final disaster. One was William Laud, Archbishop of Canterbury, an eminent and learned churchman, who did a great deal to confer beauty and dignity upon the services of the Church of England. Unfortunately he set out not only to enforce absolute conformity in England, but also to impose the English episcopalian church system upon the Presbyterian Church of Scotland. The other was Laud's friend and ally Thomas Wentworth, at one time an opponent of the King in the House of Commons, but later, after he became Earl of Strafford, his 'strong man' in Ireland as well as in England. The close understanding between Laud and Strafford, as well as the basic issues at stake, can be gathered from this extract from a letter which Strafford sent to Laud (in reply to one in which the Archbishop had complained that the Church of England was too much "bound up in the forms of the Common Law"):

> No such narrow considerations shall fall in my counsels as my own preservation till I see my master's power and greatness set out of wardship and above the exposition of Sir Edward Coke and his Year-Books, and I am most assured the same resolution governs in your lordship. Let us then in the name of God go cheerfully and boldly. ... And thus you have my Thorough and Thorough.

Strafford's concept of "thorough" government, however, was alien to English instincts and traditions, while Laud's policy in Scotland provoked a rebellion there. The King was forced to summon Parliament again in 1640, because he needed money to fight the rebels — the Crown in England has never commanded the vast private resources necessary to maintain a genuine despotism for long, and ultimately it is Parliament that controls the nation's purse-strings.

The Short Parliament (as it is known) was dismissed by the King after only three weeks, but not before another great parliamentarian named John Pym had uttered from the floor of the House of Commons the memorable words:

> The powers of Parliament are to the body politic as the rational faculties of the soul to man.

The situation was such that Charles soon had to summon another Parliament, known to history as the Long Parliament. Its assembling in the November of 1640 marked a turning-point in Britain's constitutional history. In effect it prevented the hardening of the British monarchy into the kind of royal absolutism that was at this time becoming general throughout Europe, and ensured that eventually the House of Commons, working through the Crown, would become the central source of administrative and executive power.

One of the first steps taken by the Long Parliament was to demand the trial of Strafford, on the grounds that he had plotted with his royal master to bring an army over from Ireland. Both Strafford and Laud were eventually beheaded. The institutions through which the King had sought to govern, in defiance of the Common Law, were also quickly abolished by statute, and so were various illegal and highly unpopular methods of levying taxes. In the following year, the House of Commons carried the Grand Remonstrance, largely through the efforts of John Pym ("King Pym", as some of his followers nicknamed him), which demanded both that the King's Councillors should in future be people who had the confidence of Parliament, and that Parliament should be allowed to reform the Church of England.

The King, however, was secretly preparing counter-measures. Matters came to a head when, on January 4th, 1642, he broke into the chamber of the House of Commons at the head of his guards, in order to arrest Pym and four of his fellow Members of Parliament. This forced entry was a breach of another of the Commons' most important privileges. In fact the five members had received prior warning which gave them time to escape by boat along the river Thames to the safety of the city, where support for the Parliamentary cause was overwhelming. Nevertheless, the King had made his intentions abundantly clear, and his action precipitated the outbreak of the Great Civil War of 1642 to 1646. It was a truly tragic conflict, as is the case with all civil wars, both because families were often divided against each other and also because many individuals were divided in their own minds between disagreement with the King's rash and unconstitutional policies, and loyalty and affection both for him personally and for the monarchy itself.

The Civil War began when the King, knowing that he could not count on the support of the Londoners, fled from the capital and raised his standard at Nottingham. The main centres of Royalist support, very roughly speaking and allowing for considerable overlaps, were in the North and West; the regions, that is, farthest removed from the new, bustling commercial world of the capital. His main adherents, again very roughly speaking, were the ancient aristocratic families and also the old rustic squires and minor gentry, together with their retainers, and of course, the Roman Catholics who saw Queen Henrietta Maria as their natural champion. Those supporting the cause of Parliament were as a rule the more recently elevated nobles, the gentry who had connections with the maritime enterprises of London, the majority of the citizens of the seaports and of towns with commercial or maritime connections, the yeomen of the metropolitan and eastern counties, the Londoners, and of course, the Puritans generally.

To begin with the Cavaliers (as the Royalists, with their long hair, plumed hats and cloaks were popularly known) inflicted a series of defeats on the Roundheads (as the Parliamentary soldiers, with their plain uniforms, helmets and cropped heads were called). This was largely due to the dash and enterprise of the King's nephew, Prince Rupert (third son of the Elector Frederick V of the Palatinate in Germany and of Elizabeth, daughter of James I of England), who was a born cavalry commander. But it was Parliament that controlled the most prosperous areas and the greater resources with which to maintain their troops. The tide began to turn when Oliver Cromwell, an East Anglian squire turned cavalry commander, began to organize his "Ironsides" — strictly disciplined and devoutly Puritan troops. These included cavalry, which proved more than a match for Prince Rupert and his horsemen at the battle of Marston Moor in 1644, when Cromwell and the other Roundhead commanders (in alliance with the Scots who, thanks to the diplomacy of John Pym, had been persuaded to support the English Parliamentary cause) inflicted a crushing defeat on the Royalists. Cromwell was now entrusted with the formation of a New Model Army, and won a series of victories culminating in the decisive defeat of the Royalists at the battle of Naseby, on June 14th, 1645. The King was forced to retreat from Oxford, where he had established his court, and the following May surrendered himself to the Scots at Newark, hoping to obtain better terms from them (the Stuarts were, after all, of the Scottish royal line) than from the English.

The Presbyterian Scots, however, handed over their royal captive to their allies. A period of tortuous intrigue followed, in which Charles strove to play off the Army against the Long Parliament, and both against the Scots — all of whom at this stage hoped to arrive at some sort of compromise with him. But he appeared to have learned little from his experiences, and his duplicity and evasions earned him the distrust of all parties. In November 1647, he escaped, was recaptured, and imprisoned in Carisbrooke Castle on the Isle of Wight. From there he continued negotiations with Parliament, but at the same time also carried on intrigues with his partisans in England and Scotland, which brought about a second Civil War and the invasion of England by his adherent the Duke of Hamilton at the head of a Scottish army. Cromwell marched north, defeated the Royalist invaders at the battle of Preston, and stamped out resistance elsewhere. Cromwell's soldiers now clamoured for vengeance against the King. For a time Cromwell resisted, but eventually, despairing of any meaningful negotiations with the intransigent Charles, and having first expelled those members of Parliament who opposed it, he brought the King to trial on a charge of treason. On January 30th, 1649, King Charles I was beheaded in front of his own palace at Whitehall. He died with great dignity and courage — as the contemporary poet Andrew Marvell (himself a Republican) recorded:

> He nothing common did or mean
> Upon that memorable scene,
> But with his keener eye
> The axe's edge did try;
> Nor call'd the gods, with vulgar spite,
> To vindicate his helpless right;
> But bow'd his comely head
> Down, as upon a bed. . . .

For the next eleven years England was a Republic — but in fact, as Professor H. A. L. Fisher has said:

> that final scene before the Palace at Whitehall . . . recalled the English
> people to their royal faith, and gave to Charles the Martyr, dying like
> a great English gentleman and a saint, a final absolution from his
> many faults.

Towards a New Kind of Monarchy 11

NGLAND NOW BECAME a Commonwealth, with the Long Parliament still in session and ostensibly the centre of government — though reduced in numbers as the result of a purge of various recalcitrant members. As so often happens in a revolutionary situation, though, it was the victorious army which held the real power — and they increasingly looked to Oliver Cromwell as their leader. He further strengthened his position when he suppressed a revolt of the Army's idealistic left-wingers known as the Levellers (because they wished to bring about a social revolution by levelling the more extreme distinctions of birth, rank, and wealth).

In fact Parliament could not do without Cromwell. Revulsion against the beheading of Charles I had revived Royalist sentiment in many parts of the country. In predominantly Catholic Ireland, moreover, the Civil War was still raging — until Cromwell arrived and brought it to an end, putting the garrisons of Wexford, Drogheda and other places to the sword so ruthlessly that his name is still execrated throughout Ireland. By the time he returned to England in 1650, the Cavaliers and Presbyterians of Scotland had temporarily patched up their differences and rallied round Charles, the dead king's son. Cromwell marched into Scotland and defeated one army at the battle of Dunbar. Then he turned and followed another one, which the young Charles himself was leading into England. On September 3rd, 1651, Cromwell gained one of his most brilliant victories, at the battle of Worcester — a victory which was hailed as his "crowning mercy" because it brought the Civil War to a decisive end. After the battle, according to tradition, Charles had to hide in an oak tree to escape Cromwell's soldiers. He was a fugitive for six weeks, but eventually, after many adventures, reached France safely.

Cromwell was strongly in favour of a constitutional settlement and a general amnesty. But the Rump — as the remnant of the Long Parliament was known — sought to perpetuate its own power, and Cromwell, after a series of fruitless negotiations, turned it out. Supreme power now lay unequivocally in the hands of the Army chiefs. But Cromwell himself still hankered after a proper constitutional arrangement. He summoned a Puritan convention — nicknamed Barebone's Parliament (after the name of one of its members) — but when it proved too visionary and revolutionary, that too was dismissed. Cromwell was then proclaimed Lord Protector, and a new single-chamber Parliament was summoned.

When it met, however, it began to question Cromwell's authority — and he was forced to exclude the disaffected members. Another Parliament (from which the recalcitrants were excluded in advance) was then summoned — and it offered Cromwell the title of King. He was strongly tempted to accept. It was an ironic situation. The great champion of Parliament who had been largely responsible for the beheading of Charles I, had now come to understand something of the value of kingship, realizing only too well that although power with the king alone was not a viable system, neither was parliamentary power alone; and that the well-being of the country depended on a subtle formula in which king and parliament were inextricably blended.

Republican feeling in the Army was too strong, in fact, for Cromwell to be able to accept Parliament's offer of the crown. On the other hand, he allowed himself to be installed as Protector with a pomp and ceremony reminiscent of that of a coronation, and he accepted both the fixed revenue and the right to nominate his successor, which Parliament conferred upon him. He also restored the House of Lords — only to find that when Parliament met again the two houses launched into a bitter quarrel which Cromwell could only bring to an end by yet another dissolution. Even now constitutional government remained his aim but, like many another revolutionary leader whose power rests on the armed forces, the inexorable logic of events drove him to impose what was virtually a military dictatorship, when he divided England and Wales into eleven districts, and set a major-general backed by troops over each of them.

Nevertheless, and in spite of pressure from his republican extremists on the one hand, and royalist plots and risings on the other, Oliver Cromwell had great achievements to his credit. He reorganized the national church on a much broader basis, and although various extreme sects (and also of course the Roman Catholics) were excluded, his religious policy was on the whole one of tolerance, and he curbed the persecuting tendencies of Parliament. Above all, he fully restored England's prestige abroad. At the end of the Civil War, Prince Rupert, who was as brilliant a sailor as he was a cavalry commander, took those units of the Navy which were still loyal to the King (about a third of the total fleet) to foreign ports, from which they harried Commonwealth shipping in the Channel. But the Commonwealth found a naval commander of genius in Robert Blake. He chased Prince Rupert's fleet into the Mediterranean and destroyed the bulk of it — and from that time onward British sea-power in the Mediterranean was to be an important factor in world history. Blake also cleared home waters of the Barbary pirates (and later chastised them in their own lairs in the bay of Tunis) besides winning a number of notable victories against the Dutch, the country's main trade rivals at the time.

When he became Protector, Cromwell made peace with Holland, largely because he wished to form a league of Protestant states. He also entered into an alliance with France against Spain, and sent Blake to achieve further great victories against the Spaniards, resulting in the capture of many of their priceless treasure-ships. Cromwell's Protectorship also saw the taking of Jamaica, and various land victories on the European continent, including the capture of Dunkirk. When he died in 1658, in fact, England's prestige on land and at sea, stood higher than it had done at any time since the reign of Elizabeth I.

Oliver Cromwell was succeeded in the Protectorship by his son Richard. But the country was by now heartily sick of the rule of the major-generals, and of Puritan bigotry. At the same time Parliament was anxious to escape from the tutelage of the Army. Anarchy threatened, and the amiable and peace-loving Richard Cromwell, unable to restrain it, abdicated in May 1659. He lived abroad until 1680, when he was allowed to return to England, living quietly through four reigns, and dying in 1712 at the age of eighty-six.

On New Year's Day, 1660, General Monk, Oliver Cromwell's governor in Scotland, crossed the border with his army and five weeks later entered London unopposed. He had come to the conclusion that the only way to bring the anarchy to an end was to restore the Stuart monarchy, and it was clear that the nation as a whole agreed with him. He freed the Rump Parliament from the control of the Army, and supervised the summoning of another Parliament which entered into negotiations with Charles across the Channel. On May 23rd, General Monk welcomed him at Dover; and was rewarded by being created Duke of Albemarle and appointed to various high offices. But not long after, his great task accomplished, Monk retired from political life.

Samuel Pepys, the great diarist of the period, has given an eye-witness description of the coronation of King Charles II the following year:

April 23rd, 1661:

About four in the morning I rose and got to the Abbey . . . and with much ado did get up into a great scaffold across the north end of the Abbey, where with a great deal of patience I sat from past four till eleven before the King came in. And a great pleasure it was to see the Abbey raised in the middle, all covered with red, and a throne . . . and footstool on the top of it; and all the officers of all kinds, down to the very fiddlers, in red vests. At last comes in the Dean and Prebendaries of Westminster, with the Bishops (many of them in cloth of gold copes), and after them the nobility, all in their Parliamentarian robes, which was a most magnificent sight. Then the King, with a sceptre . . . and a sword and wand before him, and the crown too . . . The crown being put on his head, a great shout begun . . .

The colour and drama of a coronation must have been a very welcome relief after the years of rule by the stern Puritans. But although all the pomp and ceremony of kingship had returned, it was — as the famous Victorian historian S. R. Gardiner once said — "a restoration of Parliament, even more than a restoration of the King". The curtailment of the power of the Crown carried out by the Long Parliament was not undone. The restoration of King Charles II was, moreover, the work of a parliament, not an imposition by force of arms; and the absolutist doctrine of the Divine Right of Kings was dead for ever.

In some measure this was due to King Charles II himself. The Merry Monarch, as he was popularly known, was indolent and pleasure-loving. But he was also good-natured, witty, and highly intelligent. He was keenly interested in scientific developments, and it was under his patronage that the Royal Society for Improving Natural Knowledge was founded in 1662. It was said of him that "he never said a foolish thing and never did a wise one". But in fact he revealed a good deal of understanding of the basic situation which confronted him. He knew that the bulk of the nation wanted peace, avoidance of political and religious extremes, and freedom to get on with their own affairs, especially if they were businessmen or merchants. With the help of the Earl of Clarendon, who, as Edward Hyde, had accompanied his royal master into exile, and was his chief minister for seven years after his return, the King did his best to moderate the spirit of vengeance that animated the first overwhelmingly Royalist parliament of his reign, which was known as the Cavalier Parliament — and which sat for nearly eighteen years. When, for instance, this Parliament demanded retribution against those who had signed his father's death-warrant, the King — who at his restoration had promised indemnity to the former enemies of the Crown — managed to save most of the regicides from execution.

The King and his ministers were less successful in moderating religious passions. The King himself had a vested interest in toleration, in that he secretly favoured Roman Catholicism, but he was also genuinely tolerant by nature. The Cavalier Parliament, however, in its desire for vengeance against the hated Puritans, passed severe laws against all those who refused to conform to the Church of England—now set up very much on the Anglican or High Church lines that had been laid down by Archbishop Laud. On several occasions the King checked the persecution by means of royal Declarations of Indulgence, but Parliament insisted that these were illegal, and carried further repressive legislation against Dissenters and Catholics alike.

In 1665 another maritime war broke out with Holland, in the course of which the Dutch fleet sailed up the Thames and captured a number of British warships. This disgrace combined with the Great Plague (in which nearly 70,000 people died), followed by the Great Fire of London (which destroyed over 13,000 houses), the persecution of Dissenters and rumours of Roman Catholic influence at Court, to produce considerable unrest throughout the country. The King dismissed Clarendon, who unjustly bore much of the blame for the various disasters, and appointed in his place a Cabal of ministers, which is sometimes regarded as the distant ancestor of the modern Cabinet system of government. The Cabal entered into an alliance with the Roman Catholic King Louis XIV of France against the Protestant Dutch, led by their Stadtholder (head of state) Prince William of Orange. Some of the leading members of the Cabal were themselves Catholics, and they entered into a secret treaty with Louis XIV for the restoration of Roman Catholicism in England—almost certainly with the knowledge of King Charles II, who had for some time been receiving subsidies from the French king—partly because Parliament kept him short of supplies.

Mounting anti-Catholic feeling eventually forced the King to abandon his Catholic policy. He dismissed the Cabal, and appointed as his chief minister the leader of the Cavalier Parliament and head of the Anglican and squirearchal party, Thomas Osborne, Earl of Danby. It was a significant appointment in that Danby was the first royal minister who largely owed his position to the goodwill of the House of Commons. He reversed the King's pro-French policy, arranged an alliance with Holland, and cemented it by a marriage of great importance for the future, between Mary, daughter of the King's brother James, Duke of York, and her cousin William of Orange. But although Mary was a Protestant, her father the Duke of York was himself a professed Roman Catholic. Furthermore, as King Charles II had no legitimate heir by his Portuguese Queen, Catherine of Braganza, the Duke was next in line to the throne. This was the issue that above all others now threw the whole country into turmoil, and out of the struggle emerged the two great political parties which were to dominate English political life for many years to come.

To simplify a very complex situation: the Cavalier Parliament (its composition modified over the years by by-elections and various other factors) now split into two main factions. On the one hand were the exclusionists — those who wanted to exclude the Roman Catholic Duke of York from the throne; and on the other hand were the anti-exclusionists, who thought that as the rightful heir (and in the interests of the continuity of the monarchy) the Duke should succeed his brother, though under some form of limitation that would preserve the Church of England. It was about this time that the terms 'Tory' (originally applied to an Irish Roman Catholic bandit or marauder) and 'Whig' (originally applied to a Scottish Calvinistic zealot) began to be used for the anti-exclusionist party and the exclusionist party respectively.

The Whigs, under the leadership of the Earl of Shaftesbury, took advantage of the panic caused by a purported Roman Catholic plot (falsely concocted by Titus Oates in 1678) to assassinate the King, seize power with the help of the French, and massacre the Protestants. They secured the dismissal of Danby and his imprisonment in the Tower. The Whigs and their leader Shaftesbury were now supreme, especially after the final dissolution of the Cavalier Parliament and the election of three predominantly Whig Parliaments. They initiated a reign of terror against their opponents, and the Tories countered violence with violence. Eventually the King dissolved the third Whig Parliament in 1681. Some of the Whig leaders planned an insurrection, while a group of old Roundhead soldiers plotted unsuccessfully to assassinate both the King and his brother, the Duke of York. A Tory reaction set in; several of the Whig leaders were executed and Shaftesbury·fled to Holland and died in exile. During the last four years of his reign, the King ruled without a parliament, depending for his finances on further subsidies from Louis XIV of France, and when he died in 1685, James Duke of York was proclaimed King without any immediate overt opposition.

In fact, though, the accession of a Roman Catholic to the throne of a Protestant country made an eventual revolution virtually certain. King James II made it doubly certain by his political ineptitude and ruthlessness. He went on a mission to Rome, ostentatiously practised his religion, and (like his brother before him) became a pensioner of Louis XIV. In Scotland he persecuted the Covenanters (subscribers to a covenant for protecting the Protestant form of religion in Scotland). In England the crushing of a rebellion led by the Protestant Duke of Monmouth (one of Charles II's illegitimate sons) at the battle of Sedgemoor, was followed by the Bloody Assizes, conducted by the notoriously brutal Judge Jeffreys, which resulted in wholesale hangings and transportations. James also conferred ecclesiastical benefices on Roman

Catholics, prosecuted a group of independent-minded bishops, attempted to pack Parliament with his adherents, and by numerous other arbitrary actions made it quite clear that his ultimate aim was to overthrow the constitution and the church.

A number of leading politicians, Tories as well as Whigs, appealed to William of Orange (grandson of Charles I and husband of James II's Protestant daughter Mary). William landed at Torbay in November 1688, with a Dutch and English army. Men of all parties flocked to support him. King James II fled; Parliament declared the throne vacant, and in February 1689, proclaimed William and Mary as joint sovereigns.

And so the Glorious Revolution (as it is known) had been accomplished. It was glorious because so united was the country in its opposition to James II and his Catholic policy that it had taken place practically without bloodshed. It was a revolution because the new sovereigns had been declared by Parliament, so that the old theory of the king as divinely ordained and set apart had been finally abandoned and an effective balance between regal and pàrliamentary power achieved. From 1689 onwards no British monarch ever tried to govern without parliament, or contrary to the votes of the House of Commons.

The 1689 Church settlement failed to accommodate the Nonconformists, but a Toleration Act laid the foundations of eventual freedom of worship for them. At this stage, however, there was no relaxation for Roman Catholics. During the year 1689 the exiled James's supporters in Scotland, especially the Roman Catholic Highlanders, were still active, and James himself landed in Ireland with an army of Frenchmen and Jacobites (as his English supporters were called). The Scottish rebels were mercilessly crushed; and the new king, William III, led an army to Ireland and gained a decisive victory at the battle of the Boyne, forcing James to return to France. The threat of Jacobite insurrection, however, remained. The exiled James was still recognized by Louis XIV as the rightful King of England, and his court near Paris became a focus for numerous Jacobite plots. William, with the Dutch and his other Protestant allies, was at war with France until 1697 — a war in which John Churchill, later Duke of Marlborough (and ancestor of Sir Winston Churchill), began to display his brilliant qualities of generalship. By the Peace of Ryswick Louis XIV temporarily recognized William III as King of England, but the threat from France was renewed when, on the death of the childless Charles II of Spain in 1700, the whole of his vast dominions were left to the French king, thus completely upsetting the balance of power in Europe which William had been striving so hard to achieve. War again became inevitable, and Louis XIV recognized James Francis Edward, the son of James II (who had recently died), as King James III of England.

Queen Mary II had died in 1694, leaving no heir to the throne, and so in 1701 Parliament passed an Act of Settlement. It ruled that in future an English monarch must always be a member of the Church of England and that no one married to a Catholic could ascend the throne, thus excluding the claims of James Francis Edward — the Old Pretender, as he was commonly known among Protestant Englishmen. This Act proclaimed Anne, the second daughter of James II, but a staunch supporter of the Church of England, next in line of succession. The great personal tragedy in Anne's life was that although she had borne no less than seventeen children to her husband, Prince George of Denmark, by 1701 every one of them had died. The Act of Settlement, therefore, vested the succession — in the event of Anne still being childless when she died — in Sophia, wife of the Elector of Hanover, because, as the granddaughter of James I, she was the nearest Protestant relative of the royal blood.

King William III died as the result of an accident while riding in March 1702, and the Crown passed to Queen Anne without disturbances. By now the War of the Spanish Succession was raging, and the Duke of Marlborough won a whole series of brilliant victories against the French, the most famous of which were at the battles of Blenheim (1704), Ramillies (1706), Oudenarde (1708), and Malpaquet (1709). As a result French power was broken, and eventually the Peace of Utrecht in 1713 brought thirty years of peace to Europe and (by virtue of the surrender of many overseas French possessions) laid the foundations of English colonial power.

The Duke of Marlborough had married the beautiful and talented Sarah Jennings, lady of the Queen's bedchamber, and her close friend and confidante. The Duchess used her great influence over the Queen to forward her husband's career, and for a number of years he was in effect regent of England. He and the Whig party, which he dominated, were largely responsible for the most important constitutional event of the reign — the Act of Union of 1707 by which England and Scotland were finally united. The two countries had of course shared the same monarchs since the accession of James I, but they had in effect remained quite separate states. Now Scottish members were to sit in the House of Commons, and a number of elected Scottish peers in the House of Lords.

In 1710 the Queen and the Duchess of Marlborough quarrelled, and Anne took as her new favourite Mrs Masham, a cousin of the Duchess. Largely owing to Mrs Masham's influence, the Tories, led by Henry St John, Viscount Bolingbroke, and Robert Harley (later Earl of Oxford), came into power. Bolingbroke and many other Tories favoured the accession of Prince James Francis Edward (the Old Pretender), and the Queen herself was torn between a natural inclination to see her own brother follow her, and fear for the future of her country. The last months of her reign were therefore darkened by frantic intrigues among her ministers and the shadow of another succession crisis. Fortunately for England quarrels among the Queen's Tory ministers prevented any decisive step being taken in respect of James Francis Edward. The Act of Settlement, in which the Whigs had invested their future, held — and George, Elector of Hanover and son of Sophia (who had died a few months before Queen Anne), became King George I and so founded a new British royal dynasty.

12 The Hanoverians

T COULD BE ARGUED that the modern constitutional monarchy really began with the accession of King George I. Yet to begin with it seemed doubtful whether the new Hanoverian dynasty would be able to establish itself. King George was fifty-four when he came to the throne. He never learned to speak English and only felt really at home in his native Electorate (or kingdom) of Hanover. He was well aware that purely on the grounds of heredity the claim to the throne of the Old Pretender was far superior to his own. He knew that because of this many of his subjects were uneasy about his accession. Bolingbroke, the Tory leader, was an open supporter of the Stuarts, and had fled to France to become Secretary of State to Prince James Francis Edward — though later he became disillusioned with him and the Stuart cause generally (and was eventually allowed to return to England).

King George I had been on the throne little more than a year, indeed, when Jacobite rebellions broke out both in the largely Catholic north of England and in Scotland, where the rising assumed quite serious proportions. It was, however, inefficiently led, and by the time the Old Pretender himself landed in Scotland, it had already been crushed by the Duke of Argyll, head of the great Campbell clan, and Prince James Francis Edward had to return to France. Meanwhile, in England the small band of rebels had ignominiously surrendered. As they rode south they had found to their consternation, that there was no enthusiasm for their cause. The truth of the matter was that although many Tory country squires grumbled about the accession of a German king and secretly drank the health of "the king across the water", they had little

liking for the civil war which would inevitably ensue if a Roman Catholic

The House of Hanover (1714–1837)

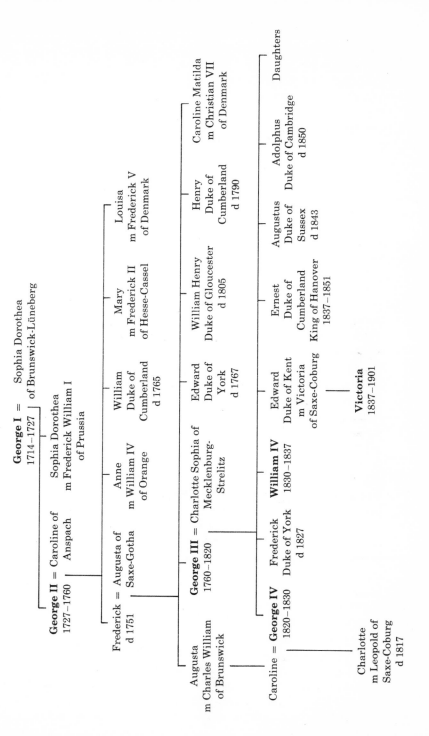

became king, while the country as a whole desired only peace and stability.

King George I was very well aware that he owed his crown to the Whigs. He hated the Tories, who had opposed his accession, and it was forty-seven years before they were again in office. It was these factors, combined with the King's ignorance of, or indifference to, English political life that led to the momentous constitutional developments which transformed the British monarchy. In the first place, since the King owed his crown to Parliament, it was inevitably Parliament which now became the predominant partner in the alliance between the two. In the second place, as the King was forced to choose his ministers from among the Whigs, and as the Whigs saw to it by various means (not all of them admirable) that they retained their majority in the House of Commons, the principle that the members of a ministry should be drawn exclusively from the majority party was firmly established, together with the Cabinet system.

The most able of King George I's ministers was Sir Robert Walpole. After the collapse in 1720 of the South Sea Company, a rashly speculative venture (sardonically known as the South Sea Bubble) in which thousands of investors, including the government itself, were involved, Walpole was called on to deal with the widespread financial chaos which ensued. Before this all ministers had been regarded as equals amongst themselves, but Walpole, although in fact he was appointed as First Lord of the Treasury and Chancellor of the Exchequer, was without doubt the leader of the Cabinet. In other words, the office of Prime Minister had also come into being. England's first Prime Minister remained in office for a record twenty-one years, and during his premiership various other prerogatives in effect passed out of the hands of the monarch and into those of the Cabinet and Parliament, among them the formation of ministries, the dissolution of parliament, and large areas of patronage in Church and state. Walpole's favourite motto was "let sleeping dogs lie", and under his leadership England enjoyed a long period of peace at home and abroad. Political and religious passions largely subsided. Toleration towards the Nonconformists, though still not complete, was greatly extended. In some degree the Roman Catholics too benefited, in that the more obnoxious of the penal laws directed against them were seldom enforced, except when fears of Jacobite conspiracy revived.

Walpole was still Prime Minister when, on the death of King George I in 1727, his son ascended the throne. King George II was a much abler man than his father. Although he too was deeply attached to his German principality, he also knew and understood England better. In consequence he took a more active interest in English politics. But it was largely due to his energetic and highly intelligent Queen, Caroline of Anspach, that the British monarchy recovered much of its lost prestige, and continued to be a powerful force. Queen Caroline made a thorough study of English political life, and exercised a considerable influence over her husband. She was a close ally of Sir Robert Walpole, and helped him to maintain his position against various Whig rivals, to preserve peace with France (and thus rob the exiled Stuarts of French support) and to avoid foreign entanglements in general.

In 1737, however, Queen Caroline died, and two years later popular clamour against Spain, which, in a brief resurgence of her old power, had attempted to reimpose a monopoly of trade with her possessions in South America, led Walpole reluctantly to declare war. His failure to prosecute it with sufficient energy brought a vote against him in the House of Commons in 1742, and he was forced to resign, dying three years later. Meanwhile war with Spain led to a continental war with France, partly because both countries were ruled by the Bourbon royal line, but even more because the commercial and colonial interests of Britain and France were coming increasingly into collision, especially in North America and India.

Hostilities soon merged into the War of the Austrian Succession which set the whole of Europe ablaze. One of the contributing factors was that King George II feared that Hanover was threatened — and in 1743 he achieved the distinction of being the last reigning British monarch personally to command on the field of battle when his combined British and Hanoverian forces won the battle of Dettingen. The war dragged on for another five years, however, without either side gaining any decisive advantage, and was eventually brought to an end in 1748 by the Peace of Aix-la-Chappelle.

In the meantime, Walpole's prophecy that a renewal of hostilities with France and Spain would lead to a revival of Jacobite activity had been fully justified. For in 1745, Prince Charles Edward, son of the Old Pretender, raised his father's standard in the Highlands of Scotland. The Young Pretender, or Bonnie Prince Charlie, as he was affectionately known, was brave and chivalrous, and the clansmen flocked to join him. The government forces in Scotland were much weakened because of the war in Europe. The Prince occupied Edinburgh (though the Castle held out), won the battle of Prestonpans, and then marched south into England. But again few Englishmen rallied to his cause, and at Derby he had to turn back and retreat into Scotland. Although he won several other engagements, he was eventually defeated at the battle of Culloden by King George II's second son, the Duke of Cumberland, with such terrible slaughter (both during and after the battle) that the victor earned the nickname of Butcher Cumberland.

For five months Prince Charles Edward was on the run in the Highlands and Western Isles of Scotland. Although there was a price on his head, none of the hundreds of men and women who were involved in his numerous adventures — as he fled from pursuing government soldiers and agents, eventually escaping to France — ever thought of betraying him. But although Bonnie Prince Charlie was to remain a romantic legend for many years to come, Jacobitism as a political force was dead. The realities of power were expressed in the confident words and rhythms of the British National Anthem which was composed not long after the defeat of the rebellion. The ultimate end of Bonnie Prince Charlie was tragically unromantic. He died a drunkard's death in Rome in 1788. In justice to all the exiled Stuarts, it must be remembered that it is almost certain that if they had been prepared to swear the necessary oaths, tongue in cheek, and to practise their religion in private (as Charles II very likely did), they could probably have retained the English throne with ease, and with full connivance of their ministers at the necessary prevarications and hypocrisies. It is to the Stuarts' credit that they were too honest in their faith to yield to the temptation.

Prince Charles Edward's claim to the British throne passed on his death to his brother Henry, a Roman Catholic Cardinal. When in 1799 the Cardinal was old, ill, and in considerable financial straits, the King of England — then George III — granted him a pension. Although Cardinal Henry Stuart never officially abandoned his claim to the throne of his forbears, on his death in 1807 he bequeathed to King George III a number of the crown jewels of the Stuart house. Among these was the ancient Scottish coronation ring. According to tradition, the conferring of this ring by a king made its recipient his 'tanist', or heir designate. It was therefore believed that the Cardinal had symbolically passed on his claim to the throne to the Hanoverian line. King George III was in fact the first monarch of the Hanoverian line to wear the royal Stuart tartan — and now of course members of the present British royal family frequently wear it when they visit Scotland.

Although hostilities between Britain and France had officially ceased in 1748, the struggle between the two powers for colonial supremacy in fact continued. In India, the brilliant general and proconsul Robert Clive gained a series of victories against the French, culminating in that of Plassey in 1757, which laid the foundations of the future British empire in India. In the previous year Britain, in alliance with Frederick the Great of Prussia, had joined the Seven Years' War against the French (again in part to protect Hanover). On the European continent British arms were far from successful, until the emergence of William Pitt the Elder (later Earl Chatham) as a great national leader. The French now

suffered defeat after defeat at the hands of Britain and her allies — in

Europe, on the high seas, and beyond them. General Wolfe's capture of Quebec in 1759 resulted in Canada becoming a British possession.

The Seven Years' War was still in progress when King George II died in the following year, and was succeeded by his grandson. King George III was only twenty-two years old when he ascended the throne, and his reign, from 1760 to 1820, was the longest in Britain, next to that of Queen Victoria's. Although he was German by blood, he had been born in London and was a sincere British patriot. He was thus the first of his line to put Hanover in second place, and the first to command general respect and affection when he came to the throne. He was also determined not only to reign but to rule, and for twenty years after his accession he devoted himself with great ability to trying to recover for the Crown the powers and privileges that had been conferred on it by the Glorious Revolution settlement of 1689, and which had been whittled away by the Whig oligarchy and the dependence of the first two Georges upon it. King George III had no wish to rescind the Acts of Parliament which had constituted that settlement, nor even to reverse all the encroachments on the royal prerogative which had taken place since and which had become settled precedents. But he was convinced that the 1689 settlement had placed the control of the executive in the hands of the king and not in those of the politicians. He set out accordingly to turn the Cabinet into a group of the "King's servants" in reality as well as in name, and to make the Prime Minister an instrument of the royal will instead of that of Parliament.

King George III began by recovering for the Crown the patronage of the state offices and sinecures, which had been taken over by the Whigs. He proved as great a master of bribery and corruption as they had been, and by these means he created his own party in Parliament, known as the King's Friends. He thus broke the Whig hegemony in Parliament, ruling to begin with through a series of carefully chosen, more or less puppet administrations which he changed frequently. He could not have succeeded in his aims if there had not been in existence a strong Tory opposition (the Tories, still suffering from the taint of Jacobitism, had not yet re-established themselves as a major party) or if Parliament had been democratic instead of being the preserve, to all intents and purposes, of the great aristocratic families who controlled, indeed practically owned, the vast majority of the various parliamentary constituencies. That democratic forces *were* at work was demonstrated by the tremendous popular agitation in the 1760s which attended the expulsion from Parliament of John Wilkes (a Whig critical of the King and his Friends) on three occasions (on mostly trumped-up charges), followed by three defiant re-elections by his Middlesex constituents. Wilkes was one of the first martyrs in the cause of parliamentary 101 democracy, and his case in effect gave notice that a reform of the franchise was ultimately inevitable, and with it further changes in the balance between Crown and Parliament.

By 1770, though, King George III had triumphed over all his political opponents and appointed as Prime Minister his henchman Lord North, who remained in office until 1782. It was during his premiership that the greatest disaster of the reign took place. The North American colonists had for some time resented the imposition of taxes by the faraway King's government in London. Their resentment found expression in incidents like the Boston Tea Party of 1773, when in protest against taxation a group of American colonists disguised as Red Indians boarded ships in Boston Harbour, and threw overboard their cargoes of tea. Although Chatham and other politicians advised strongly against the enforcement of the taxes, the King insisted upon regarding the colonists as rebellious subjects, and in 1775 his intransigence drove the colonists to open revolt, and their Declaration of Independence followed on the "glorious Fourth of July", 1776.

British military operations in America had been bungled from first to last. In 1777 the French sent help to the Americans. The surrender at Yorktown in 1781 of General Cornwallis to George Washington, the first President of the United States of America, virtually brought the war to an end. It brought to an end, too, King George III's attempt at personal rule. The House of Commons reasserted itself, and accepted without division a motion against any attempt to continue the war against the Americans. Lord North resigned in March 1782, and since that date Britain has always been governed by a Prime Minister and Cabinet responsible not to the King alone, but first and foremost to the House of Commons.

In 1783, the same year that Britain made peace with the Americans, King George III appointed the Tory William Pitt the Younger (Lord Chatham's son) to the premiership, and dissolved Parliament. The complete victory and rejuvenation of the Tory party at the general election of 1784 was in fact as much a triumph for the King as it was for Pitt. For King George III had boldly turned his back on the Whig oligarchy, realizing that the old Tory involvement with the Stuart cause now belonged to a distant past, and that it had now become a genuine champion of the Hanoverian monarchy.

Pitt became one of Britain's greatest prime ministers, holding office (apart from one interval) until 1805. He restored the premiership to the importance and independence of the royal will which it had achieved under Walpole. He finally established the Cabinet system in the form it has held ever since, as a united body answerable to an independent House
of Commons. He guarded this independence by closing the more obvious

openings for corruption of members of parliament, and by abolishing many of the sinecures that had provided an easy means for bribery. At the same time he thoroughly reorganized the finances of the country, which entered into one of the most prosperous periods in its history, especially as Pitt also maintained peace abroad. He was even in favour of a mild measure of parliamentary reform, but both the King and the Tory party as a whole were opposed to it. The outbreak of the French Revolution in 1789, and the execution of King Louis XVI and his family in 1793 roused fears of popular insurrection among Britain's ruling classes, and hardened their attitude towards any suggestion of an extension of the franchise. Pitt's somewhat ambiguous attempts to make Catholic emancipation in Ireland part of the Act of Union, which in 1801 joined Ireland to England (until 1920) also failed, partly because of the King's hostility, and led to Pitt's being out of office between 1801 and 1804.

Pitt had entered into the war against revolutionary France with great reluctance, but he guided his country through a period of great peril, when French arms — first under her revolutionary leaders and then under Napoleon Bonaparte (who became Emperor of the French in 1804) — were almost everywhere triumphant, and the threat of a French invasion of England was imminent. Pitt lived to see this danger removed, dying a few months after Admiral Lord Nelson's great naval victory against the French at the battle of Trafalgar, on October 21st, 1805.

Since 1801 George III had been subject to spells of insanity. Modern medical research has revealed that he was almost certainly suffering from a condition known as porphyria, which can now be successfully treated but which was then incurable. In between the attacks he continued to play a vigorous part in the political life of his country (as for instance at the time of Pitt's proposed Catholic emancipation in Ireland). But in 1810 the serious illness of his favourite child, Princess Amelia, preyed on his mind, and after her death in 1811, he became permanently insane. Parliament appointed his eldest son George as Prince Regent, and the old King, who also lost his sight, lived in close retirement until his death, at the age of eighty-one, in 1820.

King George III had always retained a good deal of popular affection, even during the period of his personal rule, and the loss of the American colonies. He was in many respects a remarkable man. He had a firm grasp of politics. He was on the whole an ideal family man. He was keenly interested in contemporary developments in agriculture, and his creation of model farms on his estates at Windsor, where all kinds of important agricultural experiments and improvements were carried out, earned him the nickname of Farmer George. He had a passion for music, furniture and gardens. He had, too, many curious and endearing hobbies, such as making buttons and putting watches together. He was a patron 103 of the sciences and the arts, and his fine collection of books later made a notable addition to the British Museum Library.

His son was a very different man, who brought the monarchy into much disrepute. When he was fifteen his tutor had said of him:

> He will be either the most polished gentleman, or the most accomplished blackguard in Europe — probably both.

Both indeed was what he turned out to be. As Prince Regent he was known as the First Gentleman of Europe, and in some respects he deserved the title. He was the unquestioned leader of London society, and set the fashion in dress, art, and architecture. The Regency Style, as it came to be known, was often admirable. The Chinese Pavilion which (while still Prince of Wales) he had built in 1784 at Brighton — the south coast resort which he discovered and made fashionable — and which he continued to extend and decorate for many years, is over-ornate and perhaps vulgar, but it has a decided bravura fascination — though Regent Street, one of the most beautiful thoroughfares in Europe, Regent's Park, and Regency architecture generally, are more impressive memorials. It was he, too, who was largely instrumental (after he came to the throne as King George IV in 1820) in founding the National Gallery in London. He patronized all the arts with considerable taste and intelligence. He was an admirer of the novelist Jane Austen, and it was he who in 1820 conferred a knighthood on the great historical novelist Walter Scott, declaring:

> I shall always reflect with pleasure on Sir Walter Scott's having been the first creation of my reign.

But King George IV was also the most immoral of men, and by his example turned Regency society into a byword for cynical and irresponsible profligacy. Already, as Prince of Wales, he had had numerous mistresses. In 1785 he had gone through a form of marriage with Mrs Fitzherbert, a Roman Catholic — by so doing forfeiting his right to the throne. In 1795, however, he was officially married to Princess Caroline of Brunswick — and treated her abominably. His exclusion of her from his coronation ceremony, his repeated attempts to divorce her, and the sordid quarrel between them that went on until her death in 1821, aroused

---

Page 105: King Charles I (reigned 1625–1649). His conflict with Parliament over the question of royal prerogative led to civil war and ended with his death by execution for treason.

Page 106: King George III (reigned 1760–1820). He took a more active part in government than his Hanoverian predecessors.

considerable indignation among his subjects, most of whom sided with Queen Caroline.

As Prince of Wales King George IV had called himself a Whig and affected reformist opinions, largely in order to score against his father — unfortunately enmity between the king and his heir had been a feature of the Hanoverian monarchy, and was to continue until modern times. When he had become Prince Regent, however, George had changed his opinions and backed his various Tory ministries. But he was too wrapped up in his pleasures — at a time when the whole of Europe was convulsed in the Napoleonic wars — to be seriously considered as a political force. It was Parliament, and even more, a patriotic people united in their determination to overthrow the Emperor Napoleon Bonaparte, which eventually achieved the great victories culminating in the battle of Waterloo in 1815, and Napoleon's banishment to the island of St Helena.

In the period after the war, King George IV's extravagance, dissoluteness, and frivolity were thrown into even greater relief because of the widespread distress caused by the aftermath of a long and costly war and by the terrible growing pains of the Industrial Revolution — which repressive governments, still frightened of revolution, did little to alleviate. When King George IV died in 1830, there were few who mourned him. The Duke of Wellington, victor of the battle of Waterloo, sought to do him justice, however, when he wrote:

> He was the most extraordinary compound of talent, wit, buffoonery, obstinacy and good feelings, in short a medley of the most opposite qualities, with a great preponderance of good — that I saw in any character in my life.

George IV's only legitimate child, Princess Charlotte, had died in 1817, and so he was succeeded by his sixty-five year old brother, the Duke of Clarence. King William IV, "the sailor king", as he was popularly known (because he had served in the Royal Navy, becoming Lord High Admiral in 1827), was a welcome contrast to his predecessor. Although he had lived for many years with the actress Mrs Jordan, by whom he had ten children, his private life after his marriage to a young German princess in 1818 had been exemplary. He was mild and unassuming, and hated pomp and ceremony so much that he even tried to dispense with a coronation. Although he was nothing like the equal of his brother, George IV, in intelligence, he nevertheless handled the central crisis of his reign, the passage of the Great Reform Bill, with considerable coolness and dexterity.

For some time past popular agitation for the reform of parliament, so that it would be more representative, had been growing. The reactionary Tory ministries, backed by George IV, had resolutely resisted 107 the pressure — and the Duke of Wellington (Tory Prime Minister between 1828 and 1830 and one of the chief opponents of reform) had been hooted at by a London mob on the anniversary of the battle of Waterloo. In 1830, however, the more liberal-minded Whigs were returned to office, and in 1831 introduced a Reform Bill. After various changes in the drafting of the bill and a good deal of inter-factional wheeling and dealing, the bill passed through the House of Commons. But time after time the House of Lords threw it out. Support for the bill was wide-based: the middle classes could no longer tolerate a suffrage that entrusted the government of a country urgently in need of financial, economic, and social overhaul, almost exclusively to the land-owning aristocracy; while the working classes hoped for a new kind of parliament that would redress their grievances. The popular agitation rose to fever-pitch; huge petitions in support of the bill were presented, and England was on the verge of revolution. King William IV was urged to create a large number of new Whig peers in order to swamp the Tory majority in the House of Lords. He refused to be stampeded into panic measures, but used his personal influence to persuade a majority of the Lords to vote for the bill, and thus to secure its passage into law.

The Great Reform Act of 1832 was a bitter disappointment to the working classes, who found themselves (as the result of various property or financial qualifications) still without the vote. On the other hand, the Act meant that the middle classes — including the new industrialists and skilled artisans, and the more prosperous tenant farmers — now had a share in the government of the country. A measure of democracy at least had been achieved — and it is not without significance that King William IV was almost the only sovereign in Europe, in a period of almost universal turmoil throughout the continent, who survived the advent of democracy. When he died in 1837, moreover, he was succeeded by an eighteen-year-old girl who was destined to be one of the most remarkable of all Britain's monarchs.

Hanoverian to Windsor 13

QUEEN VICTORIA was the niece of William IV and a granddaughter of George III. There was one immediate consequence of her accession to the throne in 1837, which helped to make her more of a truly British monarch than any of her Hanoverian predecessors. The Electorship of Hanover was subject to the old Salic laws of inheritance, which forbade the succession of a woman. The Hanoverian crown therefore passed to Victoria's uncle Ernest, Duke of Cumberland, fifth son of George III. England and Hanover were, in consequence, separated; and to mark the change the German arms were removed from the Royal Arms of England, leaving them as they are today.

Two years after her accession the young Queen was involved in a crisis known as the Bedchamber Plot. It was the custom for the ladies-in-waiting to come from the families of the government in power, partly in order to guard against the possible leakage of government secrets to the Opposition. When the Whig ministry resigned, the new Tory ministers expected the Queen to follow the usual precedent. Victoria, however, refused to dismiss her ladies-in-waiting, declaring in a letter to Lord Melbourne, the outgoing Whig Prime Minister:

> They are my personal friends, and not party politicians .... They
> [ie her Tory ministers] wished to treat me like a girl but I will show
> them that I am Queen of England.

She stuck to her guns in spite of the fact that by doing so she temporarily lost popularity, and the London mob shouted "Mrs Mel-

The House of Saxe-Coburg-Windsor (1837–)

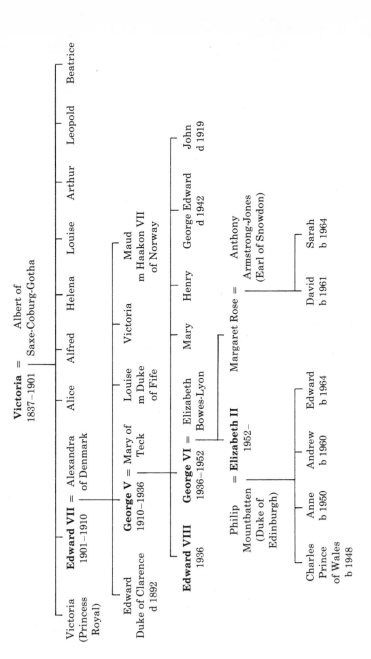

Descendants of Queen Victoria

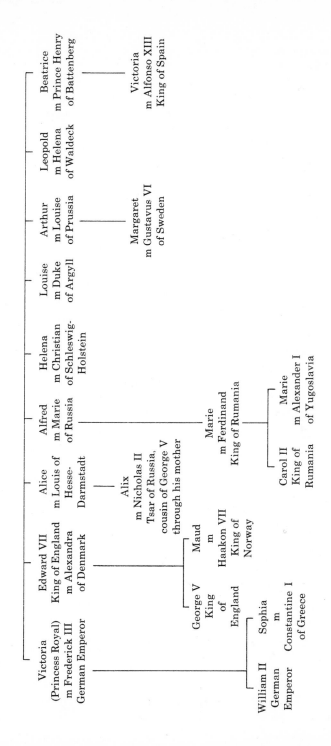

bourne" after her as she drove past in her carriage. The result was that Sir Robert Peel, the Tory Prime Minister, had to resign and Lord Melbourne's administration continued until 1841.

The incident, unimportant in itself, was significant in two respects. In the first place, the fact that a group of party politicians should be fearful of the consequences of an indiscreet word in the Queen's ear from a lady-in-waiting of the opposing party was a remarkable tribute to the personal power still enjoyed by the sovereign, and to the extent to which court intrigue might still affect party interests. In the second place, Queen Victoria's spirited behaviour strikingly demonstrated the force and independence of her character. Not that, in spite of her youth, she was likely to presume too far on her special position. She was already well versed in the principles of the British constitution, and in the first years of her reign she eagerly sought instruction and advice from Lord Melbourne. She knew perfectly well that Parliament would eventually have to be dissolved, and when the general election of 1841 returned Sir Robert Peel to power, she received him graciously and soon came to appreciate his qualities. She always had strong personal likes and dislikes among her ministers in fact: although, in the earlier part of her reign, she was so fond of the old Whig Lord Melbourne, for example, she could not stand the swashbuckling Lord Palmerston (champion of many liberal causes abroad); and later she was devoted to Benjamin Disraeli (Lord Beaconsfield)—"Dizzy", as she affectionately called him—the chief architect of the modern Conservative Party (by now, the old terms 'Tory' and 'Whig' had been replaced by *Conservative* and *Liberal*), while she abhorred his equally great Liberal rival, William Ewart Gladstone. She could be downright discourteous towards those who earned her disapproval, and especially towards Gladstone, even when, at the time of his last ministry of 1892–94, he was in his eighties and in poor health. She could also employ considerable venom in her correspondence with ministers she disliked—as in the running battle she kept up with Palmerston. She shared to the full her subjects' wrath when her governments displayed negligence or inefficiency, as when military operations were disgracefully bungled during the early stages of the Crimean War of 1854 to 1856, and again at the outset of the Boer War in 1899, or when in 1885 General Gordon was killed in Khartoum by soldiers of the Mahdi because help from England did not reach him in time.

But Victoria never lost sight of the fact that she could no longer impose the royal will in the way George III had attempted to do. Throughout her long reign she followed the actions of her ministers with the closest attention, was indefatigable in her study of state documents and insisted upon being kept fully informed on every issue of domestic and foreign policy. When she disagreed with anything she said so, and was prepared to argue her point of view fiercely and at length. But if her ministers still persisted, she always gave way in the end, and she never attempted to reverse or alter the policy in question. In point of fact, her views did sometimes prevail, especially where appointments or the phraseology of state documents was concerned. Her advice was often of material benefit to her ministers and to the nation as a whole. A notable instance took place in 1868, when the country was in turmoil because a Parliamentary Reform Bill introduced by Gladstone had been defeated as the result of a revolt by a group of his supporters in Parliament. Queen Victoria strongly advised the new Conservative government to settle the reform question, and so Disraeli (as Chancellor of the Exchequer and Leader of the House of Commons) secured the passage of another (and stronger) bill, which removed some of the injustices of the earlier Parliamentary Reform Act of 1832 by greatly extending the suffrage, thus pacifying the country — and at the same time (as far as Disraeli was concerned) gaining much political capital for the Conservative Party by demonstrating that it had the interests of the people as much at heart as the Liberals. On other occasions, the Queen exerted her influence on the Opposition in Parliament, especially in the House of Lords, in order to break political deadlocks, and she was particularly successful in averting conflict between the House of Lords and the House of Commons when in the latter part of her reign Gladstone's Liberalism assumed a more militant form.

In 1840 Queen Victoria had married her cousin, Prince Albert of Saxe-Coburg-Gotha, and for many years she was greatly helped in the execution of her duties by her adored husband. He immediately exercised a calming influence upon her, while the evident happiness of their exemplary family life, in such marked contrast to that of a number of the Queen's predecessors, and especially of George IV, soon restored dignity and respect to the monarchy. It did not, however, bring Albert himself much personal popularity. Rather stiff and pedantic in manner and approach, he was resented by many John Bullish Englishmen as a typical German. The attitude towards him taken by the ruling circles, jealous of the integrity of the British constitution, was grudging in the extreme. The Archbishop of Canterbury maintained that there was no precedent for his being included in the prayers for the royal family which form part of the Church of England services. He was excluded from any official position in the political life of the country, and although he was made a British citizen (and the title of Consort of Her Most Gracious Majesty was conferred on him in 1842) he was never granted the titular dignity of an English peer. It was not until 1857, when he and Queen Victoria had been married for seventeen years, that he was created Prince Consort. He accepted the situation quietly and with dignity. He regarded himself, in his own words, as "permanent private secretary and adviser to the Queen". But in that capacity he worked with tremendous application, and in fact exercised a considerable influence on politics behind the scenes.

As far as foreign affairs were concerned, this influence was not always in harmony with the policies of the British government. Inevitably Prince Albert was much involved with the dynastic interests of his various European relatives, and inevitably, too, he involved his wife in them. During and after the 1848 revolutions in Europe, for instance, they supported the various ruling houses, and they clashed with Palmerston because of his opposition to the despotisms of Austria, Russia, Naples, and Rome, and the sympathy and support he extended towards their victims, particularly in Hungary and Italy (then part of the Austrian empire). Victoria and Albert were strongly opposed, in consequence, to the crucial support given by the British government, under Palmerston's premiership, to the movement for Italian independence from Austrian rule, which culminated in the defeat of the Austrians in 1859, the proclamation in 1861 of Victor Emmanuel II of Sardinia and Piedmont as King of Italy, and the eventual unification of all Italy under his rule. Three years after her husband's death the Queen was involved in another clash with Palmerston when in 1864 he supported Denmark (unsuccessfully in this case) in her claim to Schleswig-Holstein against Prussia and her Austrian allies.

It has been said, indeed, that the corner-stone of Prince Albert's foreign policy was support for Prussia, then rapidly growing in strength under the guidance of her able Chancellor, Count Bismarck. This support was cemented by the marriage in 1858 of the Princess Royal (also named Victoria), the eldest daughter of Queen Victoria and Prince Albert, to Frederick, only son of King William I of Prussia. It has been argued that the pro-Prussian policy of Prince Albert was a dangerous one, because it encouraged the aggrandizement of Prussia, which — first by the overthrow of Austria in 1866 and then by the defeat of the French Emperor Napolean III in 1871 — became the most powerful nation on the continent of Europe, and increasingly a threat to Britain and her Empire. But in fact, the marriage of Princess Victoria to the Crown Prince Frederick was very much to Britain's advantage, thanks largely to the constant and detailed stream of advice from both her parents, and it became a vital focus of British interests at the Prussian Court. The Crown Prince was a liberal who strongly opposed Bismarck's reactionary policies in relation to constitutional questions and the press — and he had a horror of war. He succeeded his father as Emperor of Germany in 1888, but unfortunately for the future of Europe, he died shortly after. But his widow did her best
114 to protect British interests and to exercise a moderating influence on

her son, the Emperor William II (the Kaiser, as he is generally known in England), until her death in 1901 — the same year in which her mother died.

Prince Albert's advice on foreign policy, moreover, was often shrewd and far-sighted. The most dramatic example, perhaps, was in 1861, during the first year of the American Civil War between the northern and southern states of the union. An over-zealous naval officer of the northern forces had seized two envoys of the southern states off the British steamship *Trent*, while she was sailing between two neutral ports. The British government reacted vigorously, and war nearly resulted. The restraining influence of the Prince Consort (who was virtually on his death-bed at the time) enabled the incident to be settled peaceably, and the two envoys were surrendered to the British.

On home affairs the Prince Consort's impact was almost invariably beneficent. He understood the powers and limitations of constitutional monarchy as well as the Queen herself did. He guided her through the most difficult period of her reign, the Hungry Forties, as it was called, because of the widespread distress among the industrial working classes, a distress which gave rise to Chartism, one of the most genuinely revolutionary movements in English history. It was named after the Charter which was drawn up by its leaders, and which demanded, among other things, an extension of the suffrage to give the working classes adequate representation in Parliament.

With the advent of greater general prosperity Chartism gradually flickered out. But the serious threat it had represented accelerated the passage through Parliament of various Factory Acts and other legislation, which brought about some much needed improvements in social conditions. The Chartists' political aims were partially achieved by Disraeli's Parliamentary Reform Act of 1867, and more fully by Gladstone's Third Reform Bill of 1884. All these developments had the blessing of Queen Victoria and the Prince Consort. In some respects, indeed, Prince Albert was more liberal than many of the Liberal ministers themselves. He was, for instance, in favour of free primary education, long before it was introduced into Britain by the Education Act of 1870.

The Prince Consort was keenly interested in contemporary developments in the sciences, especially geology and mechanics, and in architecture and engineering. He strongly supported the Crystal Palace Exhibition of 1851, which displayed all sorts of examples of British technology, was an important boost to Britain's overseas trade, and was visited by at least six million people. On the Prince Consort's initiative, part of the profits were used to buy land in Kensington to be developed as a shrine to the arts and sciences. On this land were eventually built the Victoria and Albert Museum, the Science Museum, the Imperial College of Science and Technology and — a tribute to Albert's devotion to music — the Royal College of Music and the Royal Albert Hall — more fitting memorials, perhaps, than the huge, ornate Albert Monument which Queen Victoria had erected in near-by Kensington Gardens after his death.

Prince Albert was also much interested in the traditions of the British Army, in attending their manoeuvres and ceremonials, and in the designing of uniforms and decorations. One of his minor legacies to the British people was the Christmas tree, which he introduced from Germany — one worth noting because it can be seen as symbolizing the best kind of Victorian domestic contentment, of which the Prince Consort and his family were such outstanding representatives.

The Queen was heartbroken when he died. "It was the first grief he caused me," she once said. In her grief she withdrew for many years from public life, mostly to the seclusion of Balmoral, her castle in the Scottish Highlands, to Osborne, her country-house on the Isle of Wight, or to her palace at Windsor. So complete was the seclusion of "the widow of Balmoral" during the early years of her mourning that at one time she incurred a good deal of unpopularity, though by the time of her Golden Jubilee celebrations in 1887 she was again in the favour of a public who increasingly saw her as a symbol of Britain's growing wealth and power.

She was by no means idle during her retirement. Although she never again played so active a part in the political life of the nation, she continued conscientiously to study all state papers and to insist upon being kept fully informed of affairs, and she never neglected any of her essential duties as Queen. In addition, she maintained a voluminous correspondence with her numerous relatives. This in itself was no trivial contribution to the nation's well-being. Apart from the Crimean War (during which she introduced the Victoria Cross, Britain's highest award for valour in battle) England was involved in no major European conflict between 1815 and the outbreak of the First World War in 1914 — and Queen Victoria's family connections, increasingly complex as she grew older and her children and grandchildren married, undoubtedly played a part in preserving the peace of Europe. She was in effect the head of a vast international royal family, and she ruled it like a true Victorian matriarch. She was related, either directly or by marriage, to the royal houses of Germany, Russia, Greece, Rumania, Sweden, Denmark, Norway, Belgium, and Spain, as well as to those of several minor German principalities. It was no small matter that the mighty Tsar of All the Russias was "dear Nicky", her grandson; or that another grandson, the dreaded Kaiser, William II of Germany, was to her plain "Willy". In a sense, it brought them all together and to some extent at any rate, it
116 brought the great issues they represented down to scale.

Part of the secret of the spell increasingly exercised by Queen Victoria was, indeed, the element of simple, even humdrum ordinariness in her make-up. She did not mix much with the old English aristocracy, and they tended to look down on her. Her tastes, when once the influence of the Prince Consort was removed, were incorrigibly middle class. She had the typical middle-class dislike of 'modern' painting and music — on one occasion she commented on a drinking-song by Rubinstein: "You couldn't drink a cup of tea to that." The consequence was that although she could also be a very queenly, not to say imperious figure, the mass of her subjects were able to identify with her. The number of these subjects increased enormously, of course, during her reign, in view of the fact that the British Empire more than doubled in size. New Zealand was annexed in 1840, while Canada became a Dominion in 1867, and Australia a Commonwealth in 1900. In 1858, following the Indian Mutiny, the old East India Company, which up to that date had been nominally in control of India, was replaced by direct British administration.

At that stage imperialism as a conscious doctrine had hardly begun: there were many who distrusted it, and many who, throughout the nineteenth century, found it repugnant. As time went by, however, expansionist policies prevailed, dictated mainly by commercial interests but increasingly accompanied (and rationalized) by an imperialist mystique. The rest of India and then Burma were conquered. The British Empire reached out to the Pacific, South Africa and other parts of the African continent. In 1875 the Prime Minister Disraeli, who in 1852 had expressed the earlier attitude when he spoke of "these wretched colonies" as "a millstone round our necks", acquired virtual control of the Suez Canal, for many years a vital link in the consolidation of the British Empire, bringing Egypt and later the Sudan into its orbit.

Nevertheless, it was only gradually that the imperial concept of the British Crown came into being, and it was not until 1876 that Queen Victoria, on the prompting of her ministers, added to her titles that of Empress of India. Many of the psychological effects of the new imperialism upon the British people, and above all the spirit of jingoism and racial intolerance which it only too often bred, can only be deplored. But at least it can be said of Queen Victoria that she frequently showed herself less prone to them than many of her subjects or even her ministers. After the Indian Mutiny of 1857, for instance, she expressed, in a letter to the Governor-General, her:

> feelings of sorrow and indignation at the un-Christian spirit shown, alas, to a great extent by the public towards Indians in general.

She always displayed a special aptitude, attended by courteous consideration, in dealing with her imperial subjects of other races, and in one of her memoranda to her ministers she insisted that as far as she was concerned her Indian and other Asiatic subjects

> should know that there is no hatred to a brown skin — none; but the greatest wish on their Queen's part to see them happy, contented and flourishing.

This sort of attitude on the part of the Queen may help to explain why her Diamond Jubilee in 1897 (the sixtieth anniversary of her accession to the throne) was an occasion for celebration not only in Britain but also throughout the Empire. The last years of her reign, though, were overshadowed by increasing tension in Europe, as other great powers, and especially Germany, joined in the colonial scramble, and by the Boer War, which began in October 1899 with disastrous defeats for the British troops. These defeats raised British jingoism to fever-pitch, but it was bitterly opposed by many liberal-minded Englishmen, to whom the reverses seemed a punishment for imperial *hubris*. Eventually British arms prevailed, and the war was brought to an end in May 1902.

Queen Victoria herself did not live to see it. She died at Osborne on January 22nd, 1901, in the sixty-fourth year of her reign. Many of her subjects received the news of her death with a feeling not only of grief but of awe. She had lived among them for so long, that she had seemed almost immortal. She had become the very embodiment of Britain's pride, power, and stability. Her death seemed not only the end of a reign, but the end of an era.

Victoria was one of the greatest of all Britain's monarchs and she had probably raised the prestige and general popularity of the crown to their highest point since the early glorious years of Elizabeth I. The great blunder of her reign had been, perhaps, her inability to appreciate the merits and potentialities of her eldest son, Albert Edward, Prince of Wales (who was, incidentally, the first heir born to a reigning monarch since 1762). Although after his father's death, Edward relieved his mother of much of the burden of court ceremonials and public functions, she refused to give him any really meaningful official work, though he himself was hungry for it, and successive prime ministers, both Liberal and Conservative, urged her to do so. Both she and her husband had kept the Prince on a very tight rein when he was young. He was easy-going and good-natured, and his parents were evidently haunted by the fear that if allowed too much independence of action he would develop the undesirable filial features of one or other of the four Georges, or even go the way of the Prince Regent. Their distrust may have been further heightened by the fact that he tended to be liberal rather than conservative in his sympathies. He was always, for instance, deeply concerned with the plight of the poorer classes, and in spite of his mother's constant tutelage, as Prince of Wales he had indirectly lent his support to the passage of several bills designed to help them. Unfortunately the result of his parents' disapproving and repressive treatment was that, denied any real outlet for his energies, he had dissipated his great and growing powers in petty and unsuitable pursuits, and had been involved in a number of society scandals.

When he came to the throne as King Edward VII he was already fifty-nine years old and a grandfather, having married the beautiful Princess Alexandra, daughter of King Christian IX of Denmark in 1863. It was soon apparent that his mother had seriously underestimated her son. For one thing he quickly became more popular with the mass of the people than any monarch since Charles II. The scandals continued, but although these shocked the middle classes, paradoxically perhaps they were regarded by large sections of the working classes with a kind of amused indulgence. Unlike his mother in the latter part of her reign, King Edward VII enjoyed appearing in public and meeting all classes of people. "Teddy", as the populace affectionately referred to him, was also devoted to sport, especially sailing and racing. In 1909 he became the first reigning monarch ever to win the Derby, the most famous flat-race in Europe, with his horse Minoru. This may seem a trivial matter, but the British are a fanatically, perhaps ridiculously, sport-loving nation — and "Teddy's" successes on the turf, illogical though it may appear to the political scientist, forged a link between him and his fellow-countrymen which meant more to many of them than the provisions of the Constitution.

His other successes, though, were of a far more serious nature. He was closely related to nearly all the reigning houses of Europe, and exercised a good deal of influence over them — and particularly over his nephew, the Kaiser. In addition, as Prince of Wales he had travelled widely throughout the Empire, and in many other parts of the world. He was in fact very much interested in foreign affairs — and revealed a considerable flair for them. These proved valuable assets when at the end of the Boer War in 1902, Britain found herself virtually isolated. The *Entente Cordiale* with France in 1904, which brought that isolation to an end, at a time when the European situation as a whole was increasingly ominous, owed much to King Edward VII — and it is as Edward the Peacemaker that he has gone down in history.

The last year of his life was passed in the midst of the most serious constitutional crisis since the House of Lords had blocked the passage of the Great Reform Bill in 1831. The General Election of 1906 had resulted in an overwhelming Liberal majority in the House of Commons (and in the election, too, of fifty candidates of the still infant Labour Party). The Liberals set in motion the most comprehensive programme 119 of social reform in the history of Britain until Clement Attlee's Labour Government of 1945. Among the measures that went through Parliament without difficulty were those introducing old-age pensions, workmen's compensation, an eight-hour day for miners, free medical inspection of children, the beginnings of unemployment and health insurance, and an act greatly strengthening the position at law of the trade unions. But then the House of Lords, in which the Conservatives commanded a majority, began to reject several bills. Their opposition focused most strongly, though, on the Budget which David Lloyd George, the energetic and radical Chancellor of the Exchequer, introduced in 1909. This Budget was particularly repugnant to them because of its land-tax clauses and its heavy increase of direct taxation on the wealthy classes, designed to raise the necessary money to pay for the various social reforms.

The House of Lords accordingly rejected Lloyd George's Budget. There was nothing the House of Commons had fought for more energetically over the centuries than control in financial matters, and although the Lords' action was not actually illegal, it was utterly against precedent. So the Liberals countered by passing a Parliament Bill, aimed at substituting for the absolute veto on legislation then enjoyed by the House of Lords, a suspensory veto only — one, that is, subject to a time limit — and at removing the possibility of any future interference in financial measures. The Lords were hardly likely to accept this bill either, and since they had the power to force a dissolution of Parliament — and were in effect now fighting for their political survival — a general election took place early in 1910. Again the electorate gave the Liberals and their allies a considerable majority — and again the Lords refused to give way.

The crisis was still unresolved when, on May 6th, King Edward VII died. His State funeral was attended by nine reigning European kings — among them the German Kaiser — and seven queens; five heirs-apparent — including the Archduke Franz Ferdinand of Austria, whose assassination at Sarajevo in the summer of 1914 was to spark off the First World War — and many minor royalties. In all they represented more than seventy different countries. It was the last time that so large a royal concourse was to be seen together, and before so very long, many of the monarchs concerned would no longer be in possession of their crowns.

King George V was the second son of Edward VII. He had been brought up as a professional naval officer, and in that capacity had seen service in many parts of the world. It was with much reluctance that he had abandoned his naval career in order to take up the duties of heir-apparent on the death in 1892 of his elder brother, the Duke of Clarence. In the following year he had married his cousin, the beautiful and dignified Princess Mary of Teck — whose father was a minor and penurious German prince, and whose mother was a granddaughter of George III.

She was known popularly as Princess May, and she and her husband were to prove a regal and highly successful partnership.

On his accession King George V was immediately plunged into the constitutional crisis. The Lords again forced another dissolution of Parliament, and there was yet another general election. Once more the country endorsed the policies of the Liberals and their allies. Long consultations took place between King George V and his Liberal Prime Minister Herbert (later Lord) Asquith. Eventually the King adopted the same method as that employed by his predecessor William IV to force the passage of the Reform Bill of 1832, by threatening the House of Lords with the creation of a large number of Liberal peers, in order to override the Conservative opposition there. Reluctantly the House of Lords bowed to the inevitable and accepted the Parliament Bill which, besides reducing their power of veto also changed the duration of parliament from seven years to five. This meant that the Liberals could now implement their programme of reform. It also meant a drastic curtailment of the political power of the old aristocratic families (concentrated largely in the House of Lords), and a further stage in the democratization of Britain — though it did not in the least weaken the importance of the monarchy as the pivot of the whole constitutional system.

King George V, with his widely travelled background, was particularly concerned to foster closer ties within the British Empire — he was, for instance, the first reigning sovereign to visit India, when he attended a magnificent Durbar in Delhi in 1911. Like his father before him, he also did his utmost to make use of the network of family relationships among the royal houses of Europe to reduce growing international tensions. Above all he was at pains to remind his cousin William II of Germany that they shared the same grandmother. The Kaiser was by no means unresponsive. When in 1911 the King invited him to the unveiling of a memorial to Queen Victoria, he replied:

> You cannot imagine how overjoyed I am at the prospect of seeing you again. . . . You are perfectly right in alluding to my devotion and reverence for my beloved Grandmother. . . . Never in my life shall I forget the solemn hours in Osborne at her death-bed when she breathed her last in my arms! Those sacred hours have riveted my heart firmly to your house and family, of which I am proud to feel myself a member.

Family feeling, however, in a world of power politics and cut-throat commercial and imperial competition was not strong enough in itself to prevent the outbreak of the First World War in 1914. Some of the strong and often hysterical anti-German feeling that swept through Britain rubbed off on to King George V himself. In 1917, for instance, the novelist

H. G. Wells referred disparagingly to the King's "alien and uninspiring court". Wrathfully the King, who had little liking for the trappings of monarchy and who would much rather have been an English country squire or a naval officer, replied: "I may be uninspiring, but I'll be damned if I'm an alien." Accordingly, George V dropped the old family name of Saxe-Coburg-Gotha and adopted that of Windsor, after Windsor Castle, which was one of the main royal residences. It was an apt choice. The name Windsor inevitably conjures up a typically English atmosphere of woodland, green fields, river, and mellow gray stone, and it is most appropriate that so fundamentally an English figure as King George V should have been the first to bear it.

There was certainly no question of his patriotism. During the war he made several visits to the front lines in France and Belgium — and he was himself a casualty, for while he was at the front in France in 1915, his horse rolled on him and he received internal injuries from which he never fully recovered. The war, in fact, brought both the King and Queen into closer contact with the mass of the people than at any time perhaps since the reign of Elizabeth I.

The British Empire and its armed forces, from every quarter of the globe, made a very considerable contribution to the defeat of Germany and her allies in the 1914–18 war. An outward manifestation of this co-operation was the great British Empire Exhibition at Wembley (a residential suburb of Greater London) which King George V and Queen Mary opened in 1924, and which contained pavilions displaying the arts, crafts, products and so on of practically every country of the Empire. The Wembley Exhibition might be seen both as an imperial assertion, and as the swan-song of the old Empire. For in 1926, the Balfour Memorandum defined the Dominions of Canada, Australia, New Zealand and South Africa as sovereign states administered solely by their own parliaments

---

Page 123: Queen Victoria (reigned 1837–1901). Her reign was the longest of any British monarch and she became the symbol of the British Empire at its zenith.

Page 124: Buckingham Palace, the London residence of British sovereigns since 1837.

Page 125: King George VI, with his family. The King ascended the throne in December 1936, when his elder brother, Edward VIII, abdicated, and reigned until 1952.

Page 126: The Queen, Prince Philip, Prince Charles, Princess Anne, Capt Mark Phillips, Prince Andrew and Prince Edward, during the Royal Visit to Canada in 1976.

and governments — but "united by a common allegiance to the Crown". These proposals eventually became law by the Statute of Westminster in 1931. India too, if somewhat tardily, was set on the road to independence by the Government of India Act of 1935.

There were also changes in the troubled relationship between England and Ireland. The *Sinn Fein* (Erse, or Irish Gaelic, for *Ourselves Alone*) Rising of Easter, 1916, had been followed by the creation of an independent parliament in Dublin two years later, and finally the Government of Ireland Act of 1920 partitioned Ireland along religious lines, with the predominantly Catholic south becoming the Irish Free State, while the predominantly Protestant north (or Ulster) remained part of the United Kingdom. In 1921 King George V and Queen Mary went to Belfast to open the first session of Ulster's own Parliament (or Stormont). In all these changes in Britain's imperial relationships the monarchy once again proved its remarkable adaptability and its value, as an entity outside sectional passions, in smoothing the processes of transition.

This was even more apparent at home, where the aftermath of war brought massive unemployment and much suffering and unrest. This led to the formation of the first Labour government in 1924 (short-lived because it did not command a majority in the House of Commons). The King won the confidence of his Labour ministers by his unfailing courtesy and consideration, and he established particularly friendly relations with the Prime Minister, Ramsay MacDonald. In 1926 there was the General Strike, and although at one stage an undoubtedly revolutionary situation developed, there was also a remarkable degree of mutual forbearance. The King was greatly impressed by a football match, for example, which was played between strikers and police at Plymouth. He exerted pressure on the extremists in the Cabinet not to provoke the strikers unnecessarily, and he worked tirelessly behind the scenes to secure a settlement. When the government triumphed and the strikers were forced to return to work, with none of their demands met, the King again intervened with his Conservative Prime Minister, Stanley Baldwin, to urge moderation on the victors. Although there was great bitterness among the former strikers towards both employers and government, none was apparently felt towards the King.

In 1928 the last stage in the long struggle for universal suffrage was reached when women (who in 1918 had been given the vote at thirty years of age) were for the first time allowed to vote at twenty-one, the same age as men (the age is now eighteen). In the following year, as the result of a general election, Ramsay MacDonald formed his second Labour Government (though he still did not command an absolute majority in the House of Commons). But the economic depression which had begun in America following the Wall Street crash, had reached 127

Britain and was soon to become world-wide. As unemployment figures soared, the Cabinet were sharply divided as to how to deal with the crisis. In the summer of 1931 Ramsay MacDonald tendered his resignation to the King, who urged him instead to carry on, with the co-operation of a number of Conservatives and Liberals. It was thanks largely to King George V, who conducted the negotiations with great skill and without in the least exceeding his constitutional powers, that the National Government was formed, with Ramsay MacDonald as Prime Minister of a coalition Cabinet. Although MacDonald's action split the Labour Party from top to bottom — as well as the by now much attenuated Liberal Party — it was in some ways an undoubted triumph for the King, and a notable demonstration of the part that a constitutional monarch could still play in the modern world.

When in May 1935, less than a year before his death in January, 1936, the Silver Jubilee of King George V was celebrated, he thoroughly deserved the enthusiastic ovations he and Queen Mary received as they drove through London — and particularly in the working-class suburbs. The King himself expressed astonishment afterwards, referring to himself as "such an ordinary man". He had not realized the extent to which the public had appreciated the way in which he had been working for the common good during a period of unusual difficulty and anxiety, or the extent to which he and Queen Mary had come to stand for standards of decency, integrity and conscientiousness in private and public life alike. Perhaps too, the Christmas Day broadcasts which he had initiated in 1932 (the BBC had started its programmes as a commercial company in 1924, proved itself during the General Strike, and became an independent public Corporation under a Royal Charter in December 1926) had played a part in bringing him closer to the people.

Perhaps the popular enthusiasm attending King George V's Silver Jubilee was also a symptom — in a period when the deposed Kaiser, William II of Germany, was living in exile, and the Tsar Nicholas II of Russia and his family had been murdered by the Bolsheviks, and when numerous other monarchs in Europe had lost their thrones — of the continuing stability of the British constitutional monarchy and of the new House of Windsor.

The House of Windsor 14

EW REIGNS HAVE BEGUN with brighter promise than that of King Edward VIII, the eldest son of George V. He had been the most popular Prince of Wales in the history of Britain. Handsome, debonair and charming, he had been allowed as a young man (though very strictly brought up by his parents and not always seeing eye to eye with his father) to mix with his future subjects to a far greater extent than any of his predecessors. He had, for one thing, been an undergraduate at Magdalen College, Oxford — and a number of tales, most of them no doubt apocryphal, were told about the President of Magdalen's pride at the honour thus conferred upon his college. When, for example, Prince Chichibu of Japan came to the college, the President is supposed to have asked him what his name meant in English, and when the Prince told him "the Son of God", the President replied, "You will find that we have the sons of many other distinguished men in the college."

During the First World War the Prince of Wales had won admiration and respect because of his persistent attempts to get round the restrictions placed on him because he was heir to the throne, and to take an active part in the fighting. He insisted on being sent to France as an army officer, and when the authorities sent him, much against his will, to a safer part of the front, General Sir Frederick Maude, the officer responsible for the Prince's safety, exclaimed: "Thank heavens he's going. This job will turn my hair grey ... He insisted on tramping in the front lines." After the war the Prince further endeared himself to every section of the public. He had a genuine hunger for contact with all kinds and conditions of people. As he himself put it later, he spent as much of his time as possible "getting to know the people of nearly every country in the world, under all conditions and circumstances". He was in fact a superb public relations officer for the monarchy. With his great personal attraction and ready sense of humour, his fondness for fast cars, sport, dancing and parties, he seemed the embodiment of the youth of the 1920s and early 1930s in their reaction against the horrors of a war in which many of them had served, and in which thousands of their companions had lost their lives. Above all the Prince had endeared himself to the working classes by his evident concern and indignation for the plight of the unemployed. While the Bright Young Things, as the young society set were called, could be seen as fiddling while Rome burned, he was obviously of a much more serious frame of mind.

When, therefore, he came to the throne in January 1936, it was confidently predicted both that he would break through the more irksome and old-fashioned aspects of royal protocol that tended to separate crown and people, and that in the economic crisis that was causing so much distress among large sections of his subjects, he would be a king to reckon with. In the event, his reign proved to be the shortest in Britain's history, with the exception of that of his fifteenth-century namesake, Edward V, who had been put to death in the Tower of London by his uncle, Richard III.

In some respects, it could be argued, it was not altogether unfortunate as far as the future of monarchy was concerned. In the early months of his reign, it became apparent that the new King was going to find it difficult to accept the constitutional limits imposed upon him. During a tour of South Wales, appalled at the poverty produced by unemployment and low wages in the mining areas, he gave his personal promise that conditions would be improved. Such a promise was quite unconstitutional and smacked of interference with his ministers, who suffered considerable embarrassment because of it. On the other hand, it certainly enhanced the King's popularity among the working classes, and especially among the Welsh miners; at the very least, they felt, it convincingly demonstrated that his heart was in the right place.

The forty-one year old King Edward VIII was a bachelor. The Establishment (though this term for the 'top people' of the country had not yet become current) hoped that he would before long find a 'suitable' bride among the royalties of Europe. During the summer of 1936, however, he spent some weeks on a Mediterranean cruise with a party which included Mrs Ernest Simpson, the American wife of a London stockbroker, whose first marriage to an American naval officer had ended in divorce. Throughout the summer the world's press, and especially that of America, were full of rumours that King Edward VIII wanted to marry Mrs Simpson. The British papers maintained an absolute silence, even when in October Mrs Simpson obtained a divorce from her husband. The government had persuaded the press to adopt this course because the King had indeed informed his ministers of his determination to marry Mrs Simpson, and the Cabinet and Archbishop of Canterbury were doing their utmost to dissuade him. Although, inevitably, rumours began to spread, it was not until December 2nd that news of a direct clash between the King and Cabinet leaked into the British papers. On the following day the editor of the influential *Times* wrote a strong protest in his paper against the King allowing "his private inclination" to stand in the way of his public duties. The whole nation was aware, by this time, that serious constitutional crisis was under way.

There was, in fact, nothing in the constitution to prevent the King from marrying whoever he chose — provided the Cabinet agreed. The fact that Mrs Simpson was a commoner was therefore immaterial. Both Edward IV and Henry VIII had married commoners — and so had King Edward VIII's own brother, the Duke of York. There was even a precedent for a king's marriage to a divorced woman — that of Henry II to Eleanor of Aquitane. But that was long before either the Reformation had placed the King at the head of the Church of England, or before the settlement of 1689 had indissolubly linked King and Church within the constitution. Not only had Mrs Simpson divorced two husbands, but they were both still alive. The doctrine of the Church of England was at that time utterly opposed to the marriage of divorced persons, and indeed to the whole concept of divorce — and by the constitution King Edward VIII was Supreme Head of that Church. If, therefore, he were allowed to marry Mrs Simpson while he was still King, the constitution would inevitably be shattered. In addition, English Law does not recognize morganatic marriage. If, moreover, the King defied the Cabinet and forced it to resign on the issue, then there would be a general election in which the whole issue would have to be thoroughly publicized and discussed, with resulting damage to the status of the crown and the whole concept of constitutional monarchy.

The King was not without supporters. A party of "King's friends" sprang up, led by Winston Churchill, who pleaded that the matter should be debated in Parliament. But apart from the fact that this too would involve long drawn-out publicity, there is not much doubt that the great majority both of Members of Parliament and of the country as a whole were against the proposed marriage. There were two courses open to the King. Either he must abandon the idea of marrying Mrs Simpson, or he must abdicate. As soon as he realized this, he came to his agonizing 131 decision, chose to marry the woman he loved, and broadcast to the nation explaining his reasons for abdication.

The consequences were serious in a number of ways. The Dominions accepted the situation, but the Dail, or parliament, of the Irish Free State seized on the abdication as an opportunity to remove the monarchy from their constitution, thus becoming a sovereign independent democratic state (and at the same time adopting the Gaelic form of Irish Free State — Saorstat Eireann, or Eire). The crisis also meant that the nation's attention was occupied, to the exclusion of practically every other topic, at a time when events of great international moment were taking place in Abyssinia, Spain and Germany. There is little doubt that Britain's influence in world affairs was weakened during this period, and that the dictators, Hitler and Mussolini benefited. What is more, the prestige of the crown in Britain had suffered a severe blow, all the more severe because of the high hopes that had been entertained of Edward VIII at his accession. A good deal of disillusionment and cynicism about the monarchy was currently expressed, and there were some who believed that it would not survive the crisis.

When George, Duke of York (Edward VIII's younger brother), succeeded him to the throne, one of his first acts was to bestow the new title of Duke of Windsor on the ex-king. The Duke subsequently married Mrs Simpson, and with her spent most of the rest of his life in exile (although from time to time he visited England privately — and alone — to see his widowed mother, during her lifetime). The new King's coronation (his brother had not even had one, so soon had the abdication crisis arisen) took place in May 1937. But it was a daunting situation that faced the man who had been so unexpectedly called upon to wear the crown. Shy and unassuming he had always been overshadowed by his brilliant elder brother. In some quarters he was thought of as a nonentity, and fears were expressed as to his suitability for the throne. Apart from his devoted work in the Duke of York Camps, in which unemployed workers and schoolboys from the big and expensive schools attended by sons of the upper or wealthy classes — in English terminology called public schools — spent holidays under canvas together, he had taken little part in public life, and — like his father before him — he had been trained as a naval officer. When he himself heard the news that he would have to become king, he confided to his cousin, Lord Louis Mountbatten:

> Dickie, this is absolutely terrible. I never wanted this to happen. I'm quite unprepared for it. David [the name by which Edward VIII was known to his family] has been trained for this all his life . . . I've never seen a state paper. I'm only a naval officer, it's the only thing I know about.

To add to his difficulties, King George VI suffered from a stammer which made public speeches and appearances at the microphone a positive ordeal. It was perhaps the courage and tenacity with which (strongly supported by his wife) he grappled with this speech defect — and almost completely overcame it — which turned the tide of public opinion in his favour. That, combined with the integrity and extraordinary devotion to duty which he had inherited from his father George V, and the obvious happiness of his family life. While Duke of York he had married the Lady Elizabeth Bowes-Lyon in 1923. Although she was a direct descendant of the ancient kings of Scotland, she was a commoner — and George had in fact been the first prince to marry a commoner since the reign of George III. As Queen she proved a tremendous ally to her husband. Her charm, kindness and courtesy, combined with real diplomatic gifts, made her much loved everywhere — as they have continued to do since she became the Queen Mother. When future historians come to record the history of the British monarchy in the twentieth century they will undoubtedly have to include the influence of Elizabeth the Queen Mother as one of its great assets, and it was in no small measure due to her assistance that the monarchy recovered from the injury which it had received.

It was the Second World War, which broke out on September 3rd, 1939, that brought out to the full the quality of King George VI, and proved how baseless were the earlier doubts that had been expressed about him. Nothing could have more clearly symbolized the House of Windsor's identification with their people's war than the sharing of common dangers. The King matched his great wartime Prime Minister Winston Churchill in determination, refusing to abandon London, and declaring that if need be he would fight to the bitter end, revolver in hand, in Buckingham Palace — which was proved to be no safe haven when in September 1940, during the German blitz on London, bombs fell on the north side of the building, on the chapel, the garden, the forecourt, and the quadrangle — without, as it happened, any loss of life.

The King and Queen were tireless in touring the bombed cities and bringing comfort and encouragement to the thousands who had been less fortunate than they during the air raids. The King also visited the war fronts in North Africa and Italy. In one way or another, indeed, every adult member of the royal family contributed to the war effort — including the Duke of Windsor, who, accompanied by the Duchess, went to the Bahamas as Governor. Of the King's other brothers, Prince Henry, Duke of Gloucester, a professional soldier, was appointed Chief Liaison Officer to the British Expeditionary Force in France in 1939; the Duke of Kent was appointed an Air Commodore in the Royal Air Force — and was killed on active service. Two other relatives on active service were Lord Louis Mountbatten, who ended the war as Supreme Allied Commander in South-East Asia (and later became the last Viceroy of India), and his nephew Philip, who served in the Royal Navy, was in the crew of the battleship *Valiant* at the battle of Cape Matapan in 1941, and eventually became First Lieutenant on the destroyer HMS *Whelp*.

And the King's elder daughter, Princess Elizabeth, who was thirteen when war broke out, joined the Auxiliary Territorial Service as soon as she was old enough, and was trained as a driver. The entry in the ATS Records reads:

> No. 230873 Second Subaltern Elizabeth Alexandra Mary Windsor. Age 18. Eyes, blue. Hair brown. Height 5ft. 3in.

When a senior ATS Officer once asked the Queen if the Princess ever spoke about her training at home, she was told:

> Well, last night, we had sparking plugs during the whole of dinner.

The effect of the war, in fact, was to bind the nation and the royal family closer together than they had ever been before, and to enhance the importance of the monarchy in general. Whereas at the beginning of the war it had been little more than a constitutional abstraction, at the end of it, it was once again a tangible reality to the nation. This would not have happened, all the same, without the genuine qualities of kingship displayed by George VI. After the end of the war in 1945, he did much to help steer the country through the transition from war to peace, under a Labour government, and in the midst of great economic and social upheaval. He was largely responsible, for instance, for one of the most important ministerial appointments in the first post-war Labour Cabinet. In his diary the King noted:

> I ... saw Mr. Attlee and asked him to form a government. He accepted and became my new Prime Minister ... I asked him whom he would make Foreign Secretary, and he suggested Dr. Hugh Dalton. I disagreed with him, and said that Foreign Affairs was the most important subject at the moment, and I hoped he would make Mr. Bevin take it. He said he would ... I hoped our relations would be cordial, and said that I would always be ready to do my best to help him.

Ernest Bevin, an ex-docker, proved to be one of Britain's most effective Foreign Secretaries. In his own quiet way, in fact, King George VI had very firm convictions about the functions of the monarchy. His central concept was a moral one: he believed strongly that the crown must represent all that was most straightforward in the national character, and that the sovereign must set an example to his people of devotion to duty and service to the state. At the same time he believed that, in relation to his ministers, he must closely adhere to the three inalienable rights of the king in a constitutional monarchy: the right to be consulted, the right to encourage, and the right to warn. No sovereign could have practised more steadfastly what he preached.

The period of drab austerity that followed the war, as Britain struggled to recuperate her strength, was briefly and brilliantly relieved when, on November 20th, 1947, Princess Elizabeth married her cousin, Lieutenant Philip Mountbatten (created Duke of Edinburgh by the King before the wedding). Considering the rapidly changing social climate, this royal occasion with all its pomp and magnificence and its reliance upon ancient religious and civic tradition provided outstanding proof of the stability of the British constitution and the important national role of the House of Windsor. That this had come about was due in no small measure to the fact that the British people had come to know the man behind the monarch. The letter which he wrote to his daughter after her wedding, for example, was of the kind every father feels like writing at such a time:

> I was so proud of you and thrilled at having you so close to me on our long walk in Westminster Abbey, but when I handed your hand to the Archbishop I felt that I had lost something very precious . . . Your leaving us has left a great blank in our lives but do remember that your old home is still yours and do come back to it as much as possible. I can see that you are sublimely happy with Philip which is right — but don't forget us, is the wish of, Your ever loving and devoted Papa.

During the next five years, however, the strain of several foreign tours, of a serious fuel crisis at home, of constitutional difficulties arising from the tiny Labour majority in the House of Commons after another general election, gradually took its toll of King George VI's health, never very robust. In 1951 his left lung had to be removed, after cancer had developed. On the cold morning of January 31st, 1952, he waved good-bye at London Airport to Princess Elizabeth and her husband, who were leaving on what had been planned as a tour of East Africa, Australia and New Zealand. On February 5th the King was out shooting all day at Sandringham (the royal country-house in East Anglia), apparently in good health. But in the early hours of the next morning, he suddenly died of a coronary thrombosis.

By this time Princess Elizabeth and Prince Philip were in Kenya, 135 staying at Sagana Lodge (given to them as a wedding present by the people of Kenya) on the banks of the Sagana river in the Aberdare Forest. The message from Sandringham was brought first to Commander Parker, the Private Secretary to the Duke of Edinburgh. It was the Duke, therefore, who broke the news to his wife that her much loved father was dead, and that she was now Queen Elizabeth II.

Epilogue

T HE HISTORY of the British monarchy, like that of every other human institution (or like the story of any individual life), is full of unexpected continuities, breaks, and reconciliations. One of the most striking of these took place in July 1976, when Queen Elizabeth II attended the celebrations that marked the two hundredth anniversary of the Declaration of July 4th, 1776, whereby Britain's American colonists, in the midst of a war of liberation, proclaimed their independence of the Queen's not so distant ancestor, George III.

During her visit, the Queen addressed the Congress of the United States of America, in the old House Chamber in Washington, now known as Statuary Hall and filled with statues of famous men and women from all the fifty states of the Union. For a brief moment, a member of the British press reported, the US Congress looked like the British Parliament when, at the opening of a new session, the Queen makes her speech from the throne. There can have been very few two hundred years ago, who could have envisaged such an apotheosis. It was as if one reel of history at least had come full circle. It was a symbol both of the healing of old wounds and of present health in co-operation and understanding.

Further continuities perhaps were symbolized when Queen Elizabeth II went on from the USA to its northern neighbour, Canada, to open the twenty-first Olympiad in Montreal. That she spoke first in French during the ceremony was a reminder (as were the French names of the city itself, of its mayor Jean Drapeau and of the prime minister Pierre Trudeau) that Canada was once the scene of another great contest, between Britain and France; and it might be seen also as an expression 137 of hope that those old wounds, too, are healed. That it was Queen Elizabeth II alone who could appropriately open the Olympic Games was at the same time a reminder that she is the official head of the Canadian state, and that the British Commonwealth of Nations and its ties with the crown survive into the modern world; while the fact that she received such a cordial reception from athletes of so many other nations outside the Commonwealth, and of every colour, creed and political configuration, suggested that the international standing of the British monarchy is as high as it has ever been. At the same time, the fact that the Queen was also there, among so many other parents, to watch her daughter Princess Anne compete, as an ordinary member of the British equestrian team, meant that her presence was more than a mere constitutional abstraction, stiff with outworn protocol; it was also something wholly natural and human.

Looking back at these events now they can be seen, of course, as the prelude to the celebration of another kind of continuity — the Queen's twenty-five years on the throne. Before the Silver Jubilee Year of 1977 began she was already by far the most travelled monarch in British history. By the time she had returned at the end of March from her tour of the Commonwealth territories in the Pacific and Australasia — Western Samoa, Tonga, Fiji, Papua New Guinea, New Zealand, and Australia — she had covered another 50,000 kilometres. In the meantime, too, Prince Charles had been visiting Africa.

A brief lull — then the complex and, for the Queen, arduous programme of tours, banquets, displays and official ceremonies began. As James Callaghan, the Prime Minister, announced in the House of Commons on January 19th, 1977, the aim of this programme was to provide a combination of the traditional and the new — and to give the nation an opportunity of expressing its gratitude for "a quarter of a century of devotion and public duty".

The programme at home really began on 4th May with the presentation to the Queen of loyal addresses from both Houses of Parliament, in the historic Westminster Hall, while a week later, the Queen entertained the Foreign Ministers of the NATO countries to dinner at Buckingham Palace — the first of a number of engagements of an international character. But the month of June marked the peak of the Silver Jubilee celebrations in Britain.

By the time the Queen had been on the throne for 25 years, the words which she spoke in a broadcast on her twenty-first birthday in 1947: "I declare before you all that my whole life, whether it be long or short, shall be devoted to your service" — were fully vindicated and joyfully recognized by the millions of her subjects who celebrated her Silver Jubilee — and another landmark in the history of the British Monarchy has been passed.

Index

Act of Settlement, 94, 95
Act of Supremacy, 66, 68
Act of Union: England and Scotland, 94;
  Great Britain and Ireland, 103
Aethelred II, 31, 32, 37, 42
Aethelwulf, king, 22
Agincourt, battle of, 58
Albert of Saxe-Coburg-Gotha, prince consort, 9, 113–119
Alfred the Great, 22, 24–28, 30, 31, 38, 40, 42, 45
Ancient Britons, see Celts
Angevins, see Plantagenet, house of
Anglo-Saxon Chronicle, 22, 25, 27, 30, 32, 38, 42, 43
Anglo-Saxons, 12, 18–20, 22, 26, 32, 48, 53
Anne, queen, 94, 95
Arthur, king, 19, 20, 30
Asquith, Herbert Henry (Lord), 121
Athelstan, king, 28
Attlee, Clement (Lord), 5, 120, 134
Augustine, archbishop, 20
Australia, 117, 122

Baldwin, Stanley, 127
Balfour Memorandum, 122
Bannockburn, battle of, 52
Barebone's Parliament, 88
Becket, Thomas à, 45, 46
Bedchamber Plot, 109

Blake, Robert, 89
Boadicea, queen of the Iceni, 17, 18
Boer War, 112, 118, 119
Boleyn, Anne, 65–67, 74
Bolingbroke, Henry St John, viscount, 94, 96
Bosworth Field, battle of, 61, 65
Boyne, battle of the, 93
British Commonwealth of Nations, 2, 138
British Empire, 7, 8, 81, 114, 117–119, 121, 122
Bruce, Robert, Scottish king, 51, 52
Buckingham, George Villiers, duke of, 82

Cabal, 91
Cabinet system, 91, 98, 101, 102
Cadwaladr, Welsh king, 18, 61
Calais, 53, 59, 73
Canada, 101, 117, 122, 137, 138
Canute the Great, 31, 32, 37
Caroline of Anspach, 99
Cassivelaunus, king of the Catuvellauni, 17
Catherine of Aragon, 62, 65–68
Catuvellauni, 17
Cavalier Parliament, 90–92
Cavaliers, see Royalists
Cecil, Robert, viscount, 78
Cecil, William (Lord Burleigh), 74, 78
Celts, 12, 17–20
Charles, prince of Wales, 10, 11, 19

Charles I, 81–88, 90, 93
Charles II, 3, 87–92, 100, 119
Charles Edward (the Young Pretender), 99, 100
Chartism, 115
Chatham, William Pitt, earl of, 100, 102
Church of England, 1, 4, 11, 65, 66, 75, 81, 83, 84, 88, 91–94, 113, 131
Church of Rome, *see* Roman Catholic Church
Churchill, Winston, 6, 93, 131, 133
Civil War, United States, 115
Civil wars, England, 44, 50, 85–87, 89
Clarendon, Edward Hyde, earl of, 90, 91
Clive, Robert, 100
Coke, Edward, 83
Cole, Celtic king, 18
Common Law, 45, 83, 84
Conservative Party, 112, 113, 120, 121
Cranmer, Thomas, archbishop, 67, 73
Crécy, battle of, 53
Crimean War, 112, 116
Cromwell, Oliver, 85–89
Cromwell, Richard, 89
Cromwell, Thomas, 66, 67
Crusades, 47
Culloden, battle of, 99
Cymbeline, king of the Catuvellauni, 17

Danby, Thomas Osborne, earl of, 91, 92
Danelaw, 24, 28, 31, 32
Danes, 22, 24–26, 28, 31, 32
Declaration of Independence, United States, 102, 137
Denmark, 22, 37, 114, 116
Dettingen, battle of, 99
Disraeli, Benjamin, 112, 113, 115, 117
Drake, Sir Francis, 76
Dunstan, archbishop, 30

Eadred, king, 30
Eadwig, king, 30
East Anglia, 18, 20, 22, 31
Edgar, king of Wessex, 21
Edgar I, 30–32, 42
Edmund I, 28, 30
Edmund II (Ironside), 31
Edward I, 50–52
Edward II, 51, 52
Edward III, 52–54, 56, 58, 65
Edward IV, 59–61, 131

Edward V, 60, 61, 130
Edward VI, 67, 68
Edward VII, 118–120
Edward VIII, 129–133
Edward the Black Prince, 53, 54
Edward the Confessor, 37, 40, 50
Edward the Elder, 28
Edward the Martyr, 31
Egbert, king, 22
Eleanor of Aquitaine, 46, 131
Elizabeth I, 67, 68, 73–78, 80–83, 89, 118, 122
Elizabeth II, 1–12, 18, 19, 21, 42, 134–138
Elizabeth Bowes-Lyon (the Queen Mother), 133, 134
Elizabeth of York, 61
Ellandune, battle of, 21
Entente Cordiale, 119
Essex, 18, 20

Fawkes, Guy, 81
Feudal system, 42, 43, 50, 54
First World War, 116, 120–122, 127, 129, 130
Flodden, battle of, 63
France and the French, 48, 50, 52–54, 58–60, 63, 65, 66, 73–75, 82, 89, 91–94, 99, 100, 102, 103, 119, 122, 138
Frederick III, German emperor, 114
French Revolution, 103

Geoffrey, count of Anjou, 44, 45
George I, 95, 96, 98, 101, 118
George II, 98, 99, 101, 118
George III, 100–104, 107, 109, 112, 118, 120, 133, 137
George IV, 103, 104, 107, 113, 118
George V, 4, 120–122, 127–129, 132, 133
George VI, 8, 9, 11, 131–136
Germany, 47, 116, 118, 122, 132
Gladstone, William Ewart, 112, 113, 115
Glendower, Owen, 56, 58
Glorious Revolution, 93, 101
Godwin, earl of Wessex, 32, 37
Government of India Act, 127
Government of Ireland Act, 127
Grand Remonstrance, 84
Grey, Lady Jane, 68, 73

Hanover, house of, 94–96, 98–102, 107, 109
Harold, king, 37–40, 42
Hastings, battle of, 38, 53
Henry I (Beauclerc), 42–45, 49

140

Henry II, 44–46, 48, 49, 131
Henry III, 50
Henry IV (Bolingbroke), 55, 56, 58
Henry V, 58–60
Henry VI, 59, 60
Henry VII, 60–63, 78, 80
Henry VIII, 19, 62, 63, 65–68, 73, 75, 80, 131
Hereward the Wake, 42
Holland, *see* Netherlands
House of Commons, 3, 4, 51, 58, 67, 68, 83, 84, 88, 91, 93, 94, 98, 99, 102, 108, 113, 119, 120, 127, 135
House of Lords, 51, 88, 94, 108, 113, 119–121
Hundred Years' War, 52

Iceni, 17
India, 8, 99, 100, 117, 121, 127, 134
Industrial Revolution, 107
Ireland and the Irish, 20, 46, 48, 61, 65, 83, 84, 87, 93, 103, 127
Irish Free State, 127, 132
Isabella of France, 52, 53

Jacobites, 93, 96, 98–101
James I (James VI of Scotland), 78, 80–82, 85, 94
James II, 91–94
James IV, Scottish king, 61, 62, 78
James Francis Edward (the Old Pretender), 93–96, 99
John, king, 46, 48–50
John of Gaunt, 54, 55, 60

Kaiser, the, *see* William II, German emperor
Kent, 18, 20, 40
King's Council (*Curia Regis*), 50, 68, 84
King's Friends, 101

Labour Party, 119, 120, 127, 128, 134, 135
Lancaster, house of, 45, 56, 59–61
Laud, William, archbishop, 83, 84, 91
Leicester, Robert Dudley, earl of, 74, 75
Levellers, 87
Liberal Party, 112, 113, 119–121, 128
Lloyd George, David, 120
Lollards, 58
Long Parliament, 84, 86–90
Louis XI, French king, 59, 60
Louis XIV, French king, 91–93

MacDonald, James Ramsay, 127, 128

Magna Carta, 49, 50, 82
Margaret of Anjou, 59, 60
Marlborough, John Churchill, duke of, 93, 94
Marston Moor, battle of, 85
Mary, Queen of Scots, 68, 74, 75, 78
Mary I, 65–68, 73, 74
Mary II, 91, 93, 94
Mary of Teck, 120–122, 127–129, 132
Matilda, daughter of Henry I, 44, 65
Melbourne, William Lamb, viscount, 109, 112
Mercia, 20–22, 26, 30
Model Parliament, 51
Montford, Simon de, 50, 51
More, Sir Thomas, 63, 66
Mountbatten, Lord Louis, 132, 134

Napoloen Bonaparte, 103, 107
Naseby, battle of, 85
Netherlands and the Dutch, 75, 76, 89, 91–93
New Model Army, 85–89
New Zealand, 117, 122
Nicholas II, tsar of Russia, 116, 128
Nonconformists, 81, 93, 98
Norman Conquest of 1066, 1, 38, 40, 42, 43
Normandy, 31, 38, 43, 44, 48
Normans, 12, 31, 38, 42, 44, 48
North, Frederick (Lord), 102
North America, 81, 82, 99, 102, 103
Northumberland, John Dudley, duke of, 68
Northumbria, 20–22, 30
Norway and the Norwegians, 22, 30, 37, 38, 116

Palmerston, Henry John Temple, viscount, 112, 114
Parliament, 3, 4, 6, 8, 21, 51, 54, 55, 58–60, 66, 67, 73, 74, 78, 80–90, 93, 94, 98, 101–103, 107, 108, 113, 115, 120, 121, 131, 137
Peace of Aix-la-Chappelle, 99
Peace of Ryswick, 93
Peace of Utrecht, 94
Peasants' Revolt, 54, 55, 58
Peel, Robert, 112
Percy, Henry (Hotspur), 56, 58
Petition of Rights, 82
Philip, duke of Edinburgh, 8–11, 134–136
Philip II, Spanish king, 68, 73–76
Picts, 12, 19
Pitt, William (the Younger), 102, 103

Plantagenet, house of, 44, 45, 48, 55, 61
Plassey, battle of, 100
Poitiers, battle of, 53
Protestants, 67, 68, 73–76, 82, 92–94
Prussia, 100, 114
Puritans, 75, 81, 85, 88–91
Pym, John, 84, 85

Raleigh, Sir Walter, 82
Reformation, 46, 58, 67, 75, 131
Revolution Settlement of 1689, 93, 101, 131
Richard I, 46–48
Richard II, 54–56, 58
Richard III, 60, 61, 130
Robin Hood, 48
Roman Catholic Church, 45, 46, 48, 65–67, 74
Roman Catholics (English), 68, 73, 75, 76, 81, 85, 88, 91–93, 98
Romans, 17–19
Roundheads, 85, 92
Royal Council, 43, 44
Royalists, 85–88
Rump, the, see Long Parliament
Rupert, prince, Stuart general, 85, 89

Scotland and the Scots, 12, 19–21, 28, 30, 51, 52, 55, 56, 62, 63, 68, 75, 78, 84–87, 89, 92–94, 96, 99, 100
Second World War, 133–135
Sedgemoor, battle of, 92
Seven Years' War, 100, 101
Seymour, Jane, 67
Shaftesbury, Anthony Ashley Cooper, earl of, 92
Shakespeare, William, 56, 58, 74
Short Parliament, 84
Simpson, Wallis, duchess of Windsor, 130–133
Sluys, battle of, 53
Somerset, Edward Seymour, duke of, 67, 68
Sophia, princess of Hanover, 94, 95
Spain and the Spanish, 66, 73–76, 81, 82, 89, 99, 116, 132
Spanish Armada, 76, 82
Spurs, battle of the, 63
St Albans, battle of, 59
Stamford Bridge, battle of, 38
Statute of Westminster, 127
Stephen, king, 44

Strafford, Thomas Wentworth, earl of, 83, 84
Stuart, house of, 19, 78, 86, 89, 96, 99, 100, 102
Suffolk, Henry Grey, duke of, 68, 73
Sussex, 18, 20
Sweyn Forkbeard, king, 31

Toleration Act, 93
Tory Party, 92–96, 98, 101–103, 107–109, 112
Tower of London, 7, 54, 59–61, 68, 82, 92, 130
Trafalgar, battle of, 103
Tudor, house of, 18, 60–62, 68, 80
Tyler, Wat, 54

Ulster, 127
United States of America, 2, 81, 102, 127, 131, 137

Victoria, queen, 9, 101, 108, 109, 112–119, 121
Victoria (Princess Royal), 114, 115
Vikings, see Danes

Wales and the Welsh, 11, 17, 18, 20, 21, 28, 30, 48, 51, 56, 60, 61, 88, 130
Wallace, William, 51
Walpole, Sir Robert, 98, 99, 102
War of the Austrian Succession, 99
War of the Spanish Succession, 94
Wars of the Roses, 59, 61, 65
Warwick, Richard Neville, earl of, 59
Waterloo, battle of, 107, 108
Wellington, Arthur Wellesley, duke of, 107, 108
Wessex, 18, 20–22, 24, 26, 30, 31, 37
Westminster Parliament, 51
Whig Party, 92–95, 98, 99, 101, 102, 108, 109
Wilkes, John, 101, 102
William I (the Conqueror), 37–40, 42–44
William II (Rufus), 43
William III, 91, 93, 94
William IV, 107–109, 121
William II, German emperor, 115, 116, 119–121, 128
Windsor, house of, 122, 128, 133, 135
Witan, 21, 31, 38–40, 44
Wolsey, Thomas, cardinal, 66
Worcester, battle of, 87

York, house of, 45, 56, 59–61
Yorktown, battle of, 102